INSIGHTS
ON MANAGEMENT
VOLUME II

ADDITIONAL BOOKS BY THE AUTHOR

1. Adizes, I. *Industrial Democracy: Yugoslav Style*. New York Free Press, 1971.

2. Adizes, I. and E. Mann-Borgese, eds. *Self-Management: New Dimensions to Democracy*. Santa Barbara, CA: ABC-CLIO, 1975.

3. Adizes, I. *How to Solve the Mismanagement Crisis*. Homewood, IL: Dow Jones/ Irwin, 1979.

4. Adizes, I. *Corporate Lifecycles: How and Why Corporations Grow and Die and What to Do About It*. Englewood Cliffs, NJ: Prentice Hall, 1988.

5. Adizes, I. *Mastering Change: The Power of Mutual Trust and Respect in Personal Life, Family Life, Business & Society*. Santa Monica, CA: Adizes Institute, 1991.

6. Adizes, I. *Managing Corporate Lifecycles: An updated and expanded look at the Corporate Lifecycles*. First printing, Paramus, NJ: Prentice Hall Press, 1999. Additional printings by the Adizes Institute Publications.

7. Adizes, I. *Pursuit of Prime*. First printing Santa Monica, CA: Knowledge Exchange, 1996. Additional printings by the Adizes Institute Publications.

8. Adizes, I. *The Ideal Executive: Why You Cannot Be One and What to Do About It*. Santa Barbara, CA: The Adizes Institute Publications, 2004.

9. Adizes, I. *Management/Mismanagement Styles: How to Identify a Style and What to Do About It*. Santa Barbara, CA: The Adizes Institute Publications, 2004.

10. Adizes, I. *Leading the Leaders: How to Enrich Your Style of Management and Handle People Whose Style Is Different from Yours*. Santa Barbara, CA: The Adizes Institute Publications, 2004.

11. Adizes, I. *How to Manage in Times of Crisis (And How to Avoid a Crisis in the First Place)*. Santa Barbara, CA: The Adizes Institute Publications, 2009.

12. Adizes, I. *Insights on Management*. Santa Barbara, CA: The Adizes Institute Publications, 2011.

13. Adizes, I. *Insights on Policy*. Santa Barbara, CA: The Adizes Institute Publications, 2011.

14. Adizes, I. *Insights on Personal Growth*. Santa Barbara, CA: The Adizes Institute Publications, 2011.

15. Adizes, I. *Food for Thought: On Management*. Santa Barbara, CA: The Adizes Institute Publications, 2013.

16. Adizes, I. *Food for Thought: On Change and Leadership*. Santa Barbara, CA: The Adizes Institute Publications, 2013.

17. Adizes, I. *Food for Thought: On What Counts in Life*. Santa Barbara, CA: The Adizes Institute Publications, 2013.

INSIGHTS
ON
MANAGEMENT

VOLUME II

ICHAK KALDERON ADIZES

Founder and CEO, Adizes Institute
Santa Barbara County, California

Library of Congress Cataloging-in-Publication Data

Adizes, Ichak.
Insights on Management Vol. II

Library of Congress Control Number Pending

ISBN: 978-0-937120-31-6

Published by Adizes Institute Publications
1212 Mark Avenue
Carpinteria, Santa Barbara County, California, USA 93013
805-565-2901; Fax 805-565-0741
Website: www.adizes.com

Design and layout by Dana Levy, Perpetua Press
Printed in the United States of America

Additional copies may be ordered from www.adizes.com/store

dedicated to

Herman Gref

CEO, Sberbank Russia

CONTENTS

Part VI: Managing

INTRODUCTION

IN ONE SENSE THIS VOLUME OF INSIGHTS, which deals with management, is both true and false. True in the sense that, yes, they are "insights" provoked by immediacy and the events surrounding a moment, a news headline, a chance conversation. And, as such, they became a thought, really a flashing thought, written down at a given point in time and followed through to a logical conclusion. Hence, an insight.

But in candor I must admit that I have spent much of the past forty plus years thinking about management. I have conducted research and written books on the subject; have consulted to organizations, corporate and governmental, and tussled with concrete and very real problems surrounding issues and ideas related to management; and indeed have awakened in the middle of the night, unable to sleep, as ideas and theories about managing organizations, large and small, have played out in my mind.

The results are plain to see in many of my books and articles. So when I write 800 to 1000 words in response to a sudden idea or newspaper headline I call it an insight; but it is also informed by all the research and hands-on consulting and writing of books that have preceded this particular response.

So, for example, I urge you to read my brief comments on management education which, among other things, rate the current programs that major universities and schools of business continue to offer to their graduate students. When I read about business education and look at the curricula, I confess my anger sometimes gets the better of me. And out pours a new blog, a fresh insight. But in truth it sits on the back of earlier thoughts and considerable experience, both as a former professor of management and a present consultant to organizations and companies.

I read a story in the *New York Times* about a new business school program and start to mutter to myself, what are they doing...and then find myself at the computer writing my week's blog.

The same kind of recognition can be applied to other sections (and insights) within this volume. I have written extensively about management styles, the importance of change and especially about organizations and lifecycles. These writings are all present as separate chapters within these pages. "Don't get him started on change," my wife will tell a friend at the dinner table. And, yes, I acknowledge it: I am the preacher of "change." It is everywhere; it is inevitable; it is continuous. And organizations need to recognize this fact of life and adjust to it, build that concept into their business plans...or die. And so of course my insights on the subject continue to grow, and if you will pardon the word, change.

So, too, with lifecycles. I am particularly fond of my notion that organizations go through lifecycles just as we humans do. They start with infancy and proceed through adolescence into the prime of the their life and then begin to fade with age. The challenge for them, just as it is for us, is to find a way to change (there's that word again) as they proceed from one stage to the next. Again, my thoughts are constantly provoked by ideas and examples that touch on this concept...and you can read about these most recent insights in these pages.

Since this is a book on Management, a few necessary words are required here on PAEI. Readers familiar with my books and my blogs have undoubtedly come across this principle more than once. It is, in fact, the cornerstone of the Adizes Methodology and one of the first concepts we at the Adizes Institute apply when working to help companies right themselves.

This idea did actually occur to me one restless night when I had trouble sleeping. It struck me that not one single company I knew about, either through direct experience or knowledge gained from reading and research, had a CEO with all the necessary skills for managing a corporation. Invariably there was a weakness, at times an ignorance, about one of the fundamentals every corporation needed from the man or woman at the helm.

Of course, I realized, no one person excels at Production, Administration, Entrepreneurship and Integrating skills.

The gifted and smart CEO surrounds himself with managers who excel at one or two of these essential attributes. They form a team, a complementary team that at times engages in conflict, since each manager sees the corporate problem through a very particular lens. But the conflict is complementary, teammates pulling towards the same goal. The Production manager's eye is on the short-term problem(s). He is intent on finding the best and most expeditious way of producing goods that his sales and marketing people can sell now. A wonderful person to have in the lead position during the start-up phase of a company.

The Administrator is also a short-term manager, making sure that things run efficiently and on time, and with some order brought to the inevitable chaos. He keeps the trains running on time, only in this instance he sees that schedules are met, records are kept, and that a fair and productive way of paying employees becomes company policy.

My heart always runs with the Entrepreneurial hand on the tiller. He/she is the dreamer, the planner, the visionary, always looking down the road, where the company should go next. And, finally every organization is lost without an Integration specialist, another long-term specialist. He/she is the corporate communicator, the one who brings competing voices to the table to arrange something productive and workable for now and for the road ahead.

The great CEO is the one who realizes these managers have skills that he can count on, that are the best in the field, and, in many cases, far outpace his own knowledge in a single area. It is his effective use of the PAEI roles in the corporation, at specific moments in its growth and lifecycle that define his own leadership. This assumption of mine about the necessity of a PAEI team lies at the heart of the Adizes Institute and its methodology.

Another and final word about change. Some of you may have read these insights when they were originally published on my blog during the past two years. And now they appear slightly different. It is not your imagination. Rather it is a function of life and experience. Times change, as do situations, and as does my thinking in response to shifts in the world around us. Or, at times, to new thoughts generated by correspondence with my readers.

Finally some comments about the Adizes Institute, where I am the Director and CEO and on whose website these blogs first appeared. They are not, as I said at the beginning of this Introduction, the direct product of research and theory. I refer to them as insights, perceptions gathered from the rather extraordinary access to the world that my professional life has afforded me.

If you are a new or even a longtime reader, I invite you, as always, to respond to these fragmentary thoughts of mine.

My goal here is for a dialogue, not a soliloquy.

Ichak Kalderon Adizes, Ph.D.

PART I

❉

MANAGEMENT
EDUCATION

The Best Management Training: Where and How[1]

CONTRARY TO POPULAR BELIEF, I do not consider Harvard University to be in possession of the best management training program. As a matter of fact, I think it is the worst place to go for hands-on management training.

I am consciously avoiding the phrases "leadership development" or "executive development" because I am tired of playing with labels. If it makes more sense to you to interpret "management training" as leadership or executive or emperor training, do it. I refer to the management process as the process of taking a company from point A to point B.

You may be wondering where I noticed the best managerial experience, and I believe the answer may come as a surprise to you.

The best training ground for managerial experience is a sit-down, white-tablecloth, one-unit, personally owned...restaurant. If you can successfully manage such an enterprise, then I believe you can manage anything.

When John Chambers, the CEO of Cisco—a pretty well-managed company, wouldn't you say?—was asked where he learned to manage, he said at his dad's restaurant. I smiled; I agreed.

Why is a startup, white-tablecloth, one-unit restaurant such an enormous challenge? You actually have to manage, because you are it. There are no vice presidents to tell you what to do, or a board of directors to provide you with sound judgment. It is you, and you alone, who has to make decisions and live with the consequences. You have to notice, think, value, and deal with every aspect of management imaginable.

First, you need a vision. What is the concept? A restaurant is more than

1. Adizes Insights, August 2011.

just a place to get and eat food. What is the theme? Bistro? Casual? Heavily formal? Modern? Ethnic? To make that decision you have to pay attention not only to your personal passions or preferences but also to location, competition, and available market.

Next, you must design the restaurant: what size, how is the flow going to be, how is the kitchen going to function? The whole production supply chain and delivery flow need to be worked out.

After this, you must make a complementary team that can work well together or you will go bankrupt. The chef and the maître d', for example, must be a complementary team: front-and back-room managers. Not easy.

> **You need to control pilferage (i.e., stealing on the part of the staff).**

The maître d' has to be very (I), while the chef, if any good, should be (E) creative, yet still (P)-oriented to get food out on time, with some (I) to keep the kitchen staff going and working together. A Lone Ranger chef or a highly emotional, artistic, exclusive (E), an Arsonist, is a recipe for disaster (pardon the pun).

What makes a restaurant successful is consistency. A temperamental chef or turnover of chefs is a prescription for closing shop. Over ninety-five percent of new restaurant openings end in failure (i.e., they close).

You also must have a product line, which is the menu. What is the right combination of new vs. legacy items? How do you price it, how do you present it?

Next you need cost controls: How big should the dish be and what are its ingredients? How do you make sure it's always the same size when someone orders it? Any variation will cause you to lose money in no time. You must also consider inventory control. If you cook too much it is wasted, because a prepared dish can't be reused. However, if you produce too little, you run out of food, and you will have dissatisfied customers.

You need to control pilferage (i.e., stealing on the part of the staff). Also to be considered are the suppliers who may try, for example, to put the best tomatoes on the top and the bad ones in the bottom of the delivery box. An accountant once gave me a list of 108 different ways people steal in a restaurant. This list gets periodically updated and expanded.

Next, you have to worry about the attitude of the waiters. Do they bring their problems from home to work? You must think about whether it is necessary to have specialized staff or not (one takes orders, another serves, and another cleans the table). And how do you remunerate? Does each waiter/staff member collect his or her own tips, or are the tips pooled and shared?

I have found that running a restaurant is the most difficult entrepreneurial job. Starting a restaurant is a nightmare. Any of the above factors can and probably will go wrong—and they are just a very small sample of what it takes to manage a restaurant. I'll bet the infamous Murphy of Murphy's law had a restaurant at some point.

Eating out in an expensive sit-down restaurant is more than feeding yourself. It is an experience and any of the five senses may be involved at any point. You may or may not like the décor and the presentation of the food. You might find the place too hot or too cold, the chairs too comfortable or really uncomfortable. How about the smell and the piped-in music? How about the lighting? Is the waiter or waitress too attractive? Your spouse might object to going there. But what if the waiter or waitress is particularly unattractive? It might put you off.

The restaurant business is, as you can see, an endless amount of details where details count. Each and all. If the customer is unhappy there is a multiplier effect. Restaurant customers hardly ever eat alone. So if one person does not like coming to your restaurant, at least three more will not come. It is painful to stand at the door of an empty restaurant hoping, praying that someone will come in. (Just watch Gordon Ramsey's "Kitchen Nightmares" to see how painful it is!)

To me, if you can own and manage a restaurant, you get an incredible managerial experience. Second to none.

ADIZES AND ACTIVE
SOCIAL RESPONSIBILITY[1]

IN HIS INTERVIEW for my VoiceAmerica radio program[2] Ricardo Salinas Pliego of Mexico described how the seeds planted years ago by the Adizes Institute grew to become a forest.

The Adizes Institute and I, personally, have been involved for over fifteen years in helping Grupo Salinas grow from 2,000 to 80,000 employees, from just 50-odd retail stores to over 1,800. We have helped it develop, from scratch, the fastest growing bank in Latin America, acquire and rejuvenate two TV networks, and operate forty local TV stations, two cellular phone companies, a mining company, and an alternative energy company, among others.

But what excited me most was not just the growth of the company and how Adizes helped make it happen, but to hear about the component of social action. For me, that was most rewarding part of my interview with Ricardo.

More than ten years ago I suggested that Elektra, the retail company owned by Grupo Salinas, not limit its advertising to how its products offered more effectiveness for less money. "Do not promote only what you do and how you do it. Promote who you are, your values," I said firmly and often. "Show that you care."

"How?" they asked.

Usually companies display their social responsibilities as a value by donating money to the local opera house or the local museum of art. Or

1. Adizes Insights, October 2012.

2. "Grupo Salinas: Social responsibility in action," Adizes Methodology for Collaborative Management for Exceptional Results, VoiceAmerica Business Radio, October 20, 2012.

by not polluting the air, water, or soil. That is all good, but I suggested a company should do more.

In this specific instance, I suggested that every Elektra store identify a neglected piece of land in its own neighborhood, then persuade the city to allow the store to convert that piece of land into a sports park. Finally, have each Elektra supplier donate something of value to the park; for example, have the bicycle manufacturer donate the basketball court or benches and mention it in a plaque. The sport park would be a gift to the neighborhood from the company, but it would also promote Elektra suppliers and, at the same time, promote Elektra itself.

Ricardo says that profit is not the only goal.

But do not stop there, I urged. Have the store employees donate time to coach neighborhood kids who play in the park.

"It will create a buzz of support and loyalty for the Elektra brand more than any advertising you can imagine," I said.

Moreover, use the ElektraParks as a platform for social activism, I added. Organize local teenagers to start cleaning up their neighborhood by eliminating graffiti and dirt and garbage, all of which plague the cities of developing countries, not only in Mexico, but everywhere.

I also suggested that each of the largest companies of Mexico and Grupo Salinas set an example: "adopt" one of the less developed states of Mexico and donate managerial talent, know-how, and organizational skills to help the state.

In his interview, Ricardo told me how large those seeds have grown.

ElektraParks are alive and flourishing. And Grupo Salinas has adopted Chiapas, one of the least-developed states of Mexico, helping with schooling and, in general, with entrepreneurial activities. It has established fifty youth orchestras, so teenagers are not only caught up with sports in ElektraParks, but also have an opportunity to engage in the arts. And every top executive of Grupo Salinas has to donate time to social activism.

This is far and above the corporate act of making philanthropic donations. This is not just social responsibility. It is social activism.

Ricardo says in the interview that profit is not the only goal. Being involved in society is no less important. And this social activism has not hurt profits.

On the contrary, he says. It has made those profits sustainable.

How did it happen that the seeds of an idea grew to become a jungle? Why has it happened at Grupo Salinas and not with many other companies? The ideas are not that revolutionary.

The reason why those seeds flourished at Salinas is because the soil was fertile.

What does that mean? I mentioned at the beginning of this Insight that we worked with Grupo Salinas for fifteen years. Intensely. Grupo Salinas manifests the application of the Adizes success formula to the max.

By opening channels to discuss problems freely and without fear; by teaching collaborative problem solving so conflict is addressed and solved; by aligning strategy to structure and information systems; by aligning mission, structure, and rewards; and by applying the whole Adizes program of eleven phases, the program freed the company from internal disintegration. That released energy wasted on internal disintegration to be used for external integration. Not all of which was dedicated only to further financial goals. It was dedicated to social goals, too; to integration not only with markets but with the society at large.

Eliminating internal disintegration enabled external integration.

Grupo Salinas was recognized by the Adizes Institute as company of the year in 2012.

Contemporary General Management Education: A Critique[1]

THE FOLLOWING PAPER is based on forty years of consulting to corporations worldwide, plus experience as a faculty member teaching at business schools at UCLA, Stanford, Columbia, Tel Aviv University, and Hebrew University, as well as giving visiting lectures at the various universities where I have been awarded seventeen honorary doctorates.

Summary

Based on my experience, it appears that management education is failing to train those women and men who are relied upon to integrate all functions of management: general managers.

Management education today is focused almost exclusively on functional disciplines. The integration is left to business school graduates who have to learn the ropes by themselves, on the firing line. It is not easy. It is not right, either.

Furthermore, our focus in training and developing future leaders is on individuals, and my experience is that an individual who can perform all the relevant tasks necessary for management does not and cannot exist. Our training is culturally biased in favor of individualism and competitiveness, rather than collaboration, which is what is needed.

We are not just failing in the United States and Europe. We are now spreading this failure worldwide by opening business schools wherever there appears to be a market, causing collateral socio-political damage.

---

1. Speech delivered at the meeting of the International Academy of Management, Atlanta, Georgia on September 27, 2013.

1. The role of management

Before describing and analyzing where we are failing, let me first define what management (or leadership) is about, as I see it.

Business organizations are continuously experiencing change which is accelerating; new opportunities and threats that impact the organization are always emerging. They need to be addressed. The role of general management (leadership) is to deal successfully with those opportunities and threats: make decisions and implement them.

1.1 Decision making

We teach students, future managers, how to make decisions all right. But the decision-making procedures we teach are mostly in functional areas: marketing, finance, and human resources. Granted, general, integrative decisions are addressed in strategic planning; however, there is more to general management decision making than strategic planning.

General management has to make decisions that will enable the total organization to operate effectively (to meet its purpose) and efficiently in the short run and long run.

1.1.1 The ideal executive

General management requires someone who is strategically oriented and, at the same time, focused on detail; someone who is visionary, creative, and also a linear, logical thinker; someone who is sensitive to people, a team builder, who also focuses on producing immediate results, and manages by those results.

> *General management requires someone who is strategically oriented and, at the same time, focused on detail.*

We know from experience that we humans have strengths and weaknesses. No one is perfect. No single man or woman possesses all the personality traits, the complete managerial style, necessary for such managerial excellence. Experience tells us it is practically impossible to find and train someone, anyone, to provide this all-encompassing leadership. It is too much to ask. Such individuals exist only in textbooks.

The ideal executive we describe and try to develop in our training programs is an amalgam of the best traits of many people with different managerial styles. Such a person who has all the characteristics and qualities that the amalgam requires does not exist. People who worked closely with Jack Welch or Lee Iacocca, CEOs who have been considered prime examples of outstanding leadership, will tell you the same story: They are not perfect. They do not possess all the qualities that are necessary for managing effectiveness and efficiency in the short run and the long run.

The mistake, then, is that we train individuals, so-called leaders or entrepreneurs, and expect them to have all the traits necessary to manage organizations without fault.

1.1.2 Management as a complementary team

The managerial process requires a complementary team, a team composed of people with different, complementary styles. Business schools do not teach students or trainees how to correctly compose complementary teams. We do not teach which composition of styles are functional and which are destructive. Furthermore, we do not teach how to effectively handle the conflict that necessarily and naturally emerges even when a team is composed of people with appropriately different managerial styles.

1.1.3 How we handle conflict

It bears repeating: Whenever there is a complementary team, necessarily, there will be conflict. It can be destructive, unless leaders know how to convert the destructive conflict into constructive conflict.

I am not aware of courses at business schools on how to convert conflict from destructive to constructive action; in essence, a course on collaborative leadership. We teach conflict resolution all right. But conflict resolution removes conflict rather than harnessing it.

My experience with management education is that conflict is considered to be a negative rather than a natural phenomenon generated by change, which is constant. When we negate conflict, because of its destructive potential, we halt change. We encourage bureaucracy. We need to harness conflict, not delegitimize it.

1.1.4 Behavioral science: a substitute for general management

Conflict resolution has been the area behavioral scientists tend to focus on. By and large, behavioral science has replaced general management theory and practice in management education. My experience is that better understanding of human behavior does not necessarily mean that our graduates know how to collaborate and handle conflict constructively. Behavioral science, in my opinion, is phenomenological and not structural. Its proponents do not provide a systematic approach to the process of transforming conflicts into a positive force.

1.2 Implementation training

Making good decisions is necessary but not sufficient for managing well. Decisions that deal with change also have to be implemented.

Management education, as I have witnessed, does not teach much about implementation. It apparently assumes that if the decision is a good one, it will be implemented. We know from experience that this simply is not true.

1.3 Training staff not leaders

As a result, we train people who can analyze situations, diagnose problems, and make outstanding presentations of what needs to be done. But we fail to teach them how to take the bull by the horns and complete the process by implementing decisions that will handle change.

By and large, business schools excel in training staff people: report writers, consultants, investment bankers, hedge fund managers. Not leaders who know how to manage change within organizations, change that involves people.

Teaching general management has, for the most part, disappeared from business school curricula. Case studies do resemble general management experience, but the theory is missing in this kind of training.

1.4 Biased reward system

How did all of this happen? How did we depart from general management training?

In large part it relates to the values embedded in academia. To be promoted in the academic world one needs to publish. But there are no peer-reviewed publications I know of that will publish experience-based papers in general managerial theory and practice. *Harvard Business Review*, for instance, is not peer reviewed and thus does not count for academic promotion. Writing cases does not help promotion either. There are only a few universities that will recognize books based on the review of managerial practices as a valid proof of academic excellence that warrants promotion. As I have already said, strategic planning, which is a part and parcel of general management, does not encompass all that needs to be taught and known for general management.

By and large, the requirements for promotion at business schools are to produce scientific papers mostly based on quantitative analysis. The result is that the teaching faculty in business schools has been taken over by behaviorists who publish scientific papers based on controlled experiments whose findings have remote application to real (business) life; and by applied economists who rely on mathematics and computers to simulate reality, which again has limited application for general management.

General management deals with qualitative, fuzzy situations, and does not subject itself easily to the quantitative scientific research usually applied in the natural sciences. Over time, those who were interested in general management failed to get promoted and general management as such was removed from the curriculum for being too soft, too unscientific.

It is this over-insistence on quantitative scientific research that has caused general management education to be substituted with behavioral science.

General management is partially an art; this fuzzy component of the managerial process has increasingly disappeared from business education. Moreover, many business schools that want to be recognized for their academic excellence discourage their faculty from consulting. The result is that many business professors have very limited experience with real-life business practices and processes, so they teach what they know from books or journals they have read or knowledge they have gained from quantitative academic research studies. The world is far messier than what controlled experiments yield, and reporting the findings does not help in handling the complex and gritty reality general managers need to master.

1.5 Dysfunctional profit orientation

Not only have the behaviorists taken over management education, but often the remaining curricula are dominated by mathematicians and mathematically oriented economists. Economic theory promotes the idea that the goal of business is profits. Profit can be measured. It can be validated. And thus very elegant formulations of what should be done or not done by management can be published.

This profit-orientation bias impacts general management education today. It makes profits and shareholder equity the banner that everyone has to follow.

True, there are courses on social responsibility and ethics. But, I would say, those courses are lipstick on a pig. I suggest their impact on the managerial behavior of recent graduates is minimal. Graduates of leading business schools today end up on Wall Street, in consulting firms, in hedge funds, where the religion is profits, led by computer-based decision making and mathematical formulations.

What is wrong with this? In the unrestrained search for profits we are destroying our environment. That is what is wrong. By managing with computers we are losing the human touch, which is essential for managing, for leading organizations well. Companies are composed of people, are they not?

1.5.1 Business training as a liability

In developed countries, because of this greedy, obsessive search for profits, business is viewed as a liability. Socially conscious young people are flocking to work for NGOs, not for businesses. Those who do go into business are not necessarily at the top rung of society. Quite the opposite. Business is considered to be dirty endeavor.

Watch movies like *Wall Street*. Read opinion pieces in popular journals. Businessmen are the thieves, greedy bastards who need to be regulated and thrown in jail.

1.6 Undermining democracy

One of the ironies of it all is that, on one hand, the US sends its soldiers to fight and die for democracy, while on the other hand business schools are promoting the opposite of democracy worldwide. They champion organizations managed by an elite that enriches itself without accountability to the people it leads.

In this way business schools have become incubators that nurture economic elites who gain political power and widen the socio-economic inequality in the nation in which they operate. This has socio-political repercussions that later have to be dealt with by military power in order to overcome revolutionary tendencies on the part of those who feel exploited.

2.0 Quo vadis?

It is long past time for our business schools to do some soul searching and to reconsider the premises on which their education programs and policies are based.

What Is Wrong with Business Schools?[1]

FIFTY YEARS AGO, when I received my MBA and doctoral degrees at Columbia University Business School, MBA programs were not yet popular. Since that time, programs have grown like mushrooms after the rain, especially in Eastern Europe and the developing countries. In India, I have noticed, business schools are everywhere, and American business schools are making fortunes essentially franchising their programs.

What is wrong with that?

Schools of economics and business schools teach that the purpose of business is to produce profits. Finance theory and micro-economic theory preach that the goal of business is to increase earnings per share. So do all other courses in marketing and even human resources. The profit motivation is always there as the measuring rod of success.

Granted, here and there you can find a course devoted to social responsibility, but it functions as a fig leaf for the real program, which is clearly oriented around profit: market domination for profit orientation, etc.

What is wrong with it?

It legitimizes greed.

Making profit the purpose and goal for which a business exists, validates and justifies greed. If there were no greed, profit motivation as a goal would not be as attractive.

So what, one may ask?

To make profits companies have to create needs so they can increase revenues. Just look at the variety of products being provided just in a

1. Adizes Insights, June 2014.

supermarket. We promote meat consumption and never in the history of mankind has so much meat been consumed per capita. And what is the meat consumption doing to our environment? Do you know how much water and land use is necessary for one pound of cow meat? And how much pollution of our water resources the dairy business causes?

The result is that companies are profitable while the environment is increasingly getting destroyed.

Our standard of living is going up while our quality of life is going down.

To increase profits companies seek global sourcing of products and go where the costs are the lowest. That creates unemployment at home.

We preach democracy, go to war, and sacrifice our children's lives, supposedly to bring democracy to far-away lands only to turn around and franchise or promote business schools that teach anything but democracy in how corporations should be managed.

> *To make profits companies have to create needs so they can increase revenues.*

Representing owners, corporate governance, is not democracy. Workers who are managed have no say in who their leaders will be.

The reality is that we teach that benevolent dictatorship is the most desired leadership of corporations. That is the reality of our management education.

The search for economic returns is impacting how top mangers behave, too. The gap in salaries between top management and workers is the highest it's been since the era of the robber barons in the late nineteenth century.

The result is that we legitimize greed and then condemn it. We live in a galloping consumer society that is wasteful beyond comprehension, and preach democracy but promote non-democracy in our corporate life.

Overall I would say the system, as we know it now, is producing unexpected, undesired collateral damage. Profit seeking as the preeminent goal is a force of disintegration, which is hurting us and will hurt future generations even more.

Business schools are the swamps that breed the malaria-carrying mosquitoes.

The efforts to make business leaders more socially conscious, I suggest, are like swimming against a tsunami. After a year of indoctrination that profits are the goal to be focused on and are the basis upon which we grant rewards, coupled with the natural desire to accumulate wealth, developing social consciousness is like taking an aspirin for cancer. It might relieve the pain (i.e., sense of guilt) for a short time but the damage will continue to be done.

What about the theory that leadership of business organizations should have a host of stakeholders to consider in their decision making? The needs of the community, workers, and of the environment are not to be ignored.

It sounds nice in theory. In practice, if your competition produces better profits than you, your position as a leader might be in jeopardy.

What about the claim that socially conscious corporations are more profitable? Maybe, but note how the profit motive is driving even social consciousness as a measure of justification for the effort.

But responsible businesses practice philanthropy, you might say.

I find it ironic that Coca-Cola, for instance, finances a chair for social responsibility at a business school. A company that is feeding sugar to millions of people with dire health consequences. The same goes for McDonald's and KFC.

They are fig leaf efforts.

A new theory of management and economics is called for. One that provides for new goals to be followed, where profits are not the goal but the byproduct of reaching the desired goal.

Part II

❋

Decision Making

Decision Making and Implementation: What Can We Learn from Dion?[1]

DION FRIEDLAND is a South African businessman. Thirty-some years ago, he was a client; ever since then, he has been a close friend. I have been with him when he negotiates, when he deals with employees, and spends time with his family. I have been watching him closely and I realize that there is much to learn from him.

Dion is a very successful businessman. He started a retail store chain in South Africa, then moved to the US to build a sales training firm, then opened a store chain selling lighting fixtures. Next, he became an art dealer, and then established a fund to manage money invested in hedge funds. He also has a company that has a patent on machines that convert water into disinfectants or detergents. In between all of this, he built, owned, and sold one of the top ten resort hotels in the world, located in the Caribbean. By and large, most of his endeavors have succeeded. How did he do it?

One thing I've noticed over all these years is that I have never, ever, seen Dion angry; upset for few seconds, yes, but never angry, despite many warranting situations. He solves problems with no apparent emotions.

The guy simply has no "internal marketing," which I define as internal conflict. Internal marketing leads to symptoms of paralysis, inconsistent decision making, reversal of decisions already made, and, by and large, causes great anguish and loss of energy. Dion exhibits none of that; he decides and executes. I have never seen him not implement a decision. Simply stated, Dion has the strongest self-discipline I have ever encountered.

Many of us decide but then waver on implementation. With Dion,

1. Adizes Insights, August 2010.

implementation is prompt and reflects exactly the decision made. Here is an example: He is now sixty-seven years old. He decided that he will reverse his aging and his goal is to look and feel better at seventy than how he looked or felt at sixty. He has an eating regimen that he follows religiously. There are zero deviations. Once he decided to live in this way that was it, the decision was enforced.

> *His motto is "Why waste time brooding? Act on the problem or forget it."*

He also spends three hours every day in the gym pumping iron and doing his aerobics. He works four hours a day leading his vast holdings, managed by professional managers, using the internet and Skype. The rest of his time is dedicated to family and friends that he chooses carefully—people who add to rather than subtract from his energy, people he can learn from or laugh with.

I have never seen Dion in bad mood. His motto is "Why waste time brooding? Act on the problem or forget it."

Dion sold many of the businesses he started. "Today no one should fall in hopeless love with any business," he says. "Move on when it does not work. Stop beating a dead horse if the business is no good, and if it is good, stop digging when you hit oil."

In a sense everything seems simple black and white with him. Very (P), but also lots of (E), without all the confusion (E)s bring to the table. He is an (E), having started so many businesses, but this was not done like a typical Arsonist, who erratically jumps from one idea to the next. He (P)s his (E), in a way. If you ask him what his main priority in life is, his response is his health and the health of his family, followed by the health of his businesses. His goals are simple and well focused.

I think the cause of his lack of internal marketing is his level of commitment. It makes me wonder why most people I know do not walk their talk; they decide but their implementation is weak or often non-existent. With Dion, the uniqueness is that he implements his decisions totally and swiftly, almost effortlessly.

George Soros, a renowned businessman and investor, apparently has the same character. In his book *Soros on Soros: Staying Ahead of the Curve*, he says that the secret of his success is that he identifies and corrects his mistakes sooner than most people. This is the same principle of implementing decisions without hesitation. I find that surgeons, especially heart surgeons, have the same characteristic: There is no wavering between deciding and implementing. It is the artists and so-called intellectuals who "decide" but then have second and third thoughts, and their execution, if there is any, only vaguely resembles their initial decision.

This explains why most (E)s are not like Dion, because the excitement is in the decision making. That is where the mind is fully engaged. Implementation is pure hard work, no fun.

Diagnosis vs. Treatment[1]

T HE CORRECT DIAGNOSIS does not automatically give the desired prescription; it does not tell us what the treatment should be.

Here is a folk expression: "The fish stinks from the head but you clean it from the tail." The diagnosis is one thing. The treatment is something else.

It is my observation that we often make the mistake of assuming that the diagnosis tells us what the treatment should be. Assume you have a headache. The diagnosis is: headache. The treatment is to take a pill to treat the headache. But taking a pill does not treat the headache, does it? It only removes the pain. The cause of the headache continues.

> *"Stop telling me how much you love me. Start bringing flowers."*

Using PAEI, if the diagnosis is that there is a breakdown in integration, the treatment is not necessarily providing more integration. In other words, you cannot treat an (I) problem with (I). You have to treat it with either (A) or (E) or (P). In Adizes programs for healing organizations, a problem of disintegration is treated with more (A), not more (I).

An Organizational Developer, OD specialist, on the other hand, usually will treat an (I) problem with more (I): with discussions, with training, with "hot seats," etc.

In Adizes we establish rules of conduct—(A)—which produce (I). Behave as if you have mutual trust and respect; be on time; listen until given permission to talk; follow the road map on how to deal with conflict, etc. Lots of (A). And guess what? (I) increases.

1. Adizes Insights, March 2012.

You can also treat an (I) deficiency with (P). One of the expressions I use in my lectures is: "Stop telling me how much you love me. Start bringing flowers."

Finally, you can treat an (I) deficiency with more (E). An example is the kibbutz movement. (I have been asked to consult to them.) In diagnosing the problem I see that (I) has declined over time and people are leaving the kibbutz movement in hordes. The solution is not to have lots of (I) talk and try to convince people to stay. The solution, I believe, is that the kibbutz movement needs a new mission for its existence, a new ideology. The old reason to be simply is not valid anymore. The treatment should be new (E).

Let me try to summarize the point: All problems are caused by disintegration; by deficient (I). How did it happen? How did the system get disintegrated? It was caused by a breakdown in (P), (A), and/or (E). Thus, to treat the cause, not the manifestation, one has to treat the (PAE) roles. The treatment is in the cause, not in the manifestation.

This illumination explains why, in Adizes, we do not treat column 1 directly, and why column 1 and 6 in diagnosis are close to each other. It explains why we treat column 6 and eventually column 1, by treating columns 4 and 5, which are the various (P)s, column 3, which is the (E), and column 2, which is the (A).

Where Can We Go Wrong?[1]

A GOOD DIAGNOSIS does not necessarily mean that you are going to have a good prescription. You can have a good diagnosis and a bad solution together. Take Karl Marx's writings, for example. While reading his books, you find yourself agreeing with his diagnosis of what is wrong with capitalist societies; however, his solutions to the problems of capitalism brought misery to millions of people.

Here is another example. Barack Obama's diagnosis of the ills of American society excited millions, who then voted for him. "We need to change," he said and gave a pretty detailed analysis of what needs to change. However, his solutions have created many objections and many people feel that he is taking America in the wrong direction. Socialism is not necessarily the solution to the shortcomings of capitalism.

A medical doctor can diagnose a disease and prescribe the wrong medicine. There are many drugs that treat the same illness, and he has to choose which one is most appropriate. He might choose a good one, but it might be incompatible with other medicines you are taking.

A manager could diagnose a problem within a company and decide that the problem is a particular person. The solution to fire him or her could be the wrong solution because of improper timing. Firing the person could be analogous to shooting one's self in the foot.

A solution could be a bad one because you did not address the four imperatives: What you decided to do was sound, but how you did it was too simplistic, or the timing was premature, or the one responsible for implementing the decision was the wrong person.

---

1. Adizes Insights, January 2011.

The reverse situation could happen too. You could have a good solution, one that works, without an accurate diagnosis. Medical doctors often do not know exactly what the malady is and prescribe a medicine to "try it out." This is especially true for dermatologists. Often their remedy works but they cannot tell you exactly why.

The problem we are discussing here does not end with the diagnosis and solution. The implementation of the solution can be a problem in itself. The diagnosis was good, the solution was sound, but the implementation was faulty. Here anyone can bring up endless examples.

The implementation of the solution can be a problem in itself.

Why am I writing this? Because I found myself in this exact situation and I suspect I am not alone. I assume that if a diagnosis exists, then the job is done; from there on it is smooth sailing. The task is complete. But nothing is done until it is done, and done well, which means a solution is a "good solution" only when it works in reality. Until then, the diagnosis and the solution remain suspect. You cannot relax.

That is why a doctor may tell you, "take this medicine and if the problem does not go away call me back." She is not sure her diagnosis is the right one. She is not sure if her prescription is right. She is a good doctor.

But that is how managers should behave too. Good management is not managing by expecting but managing by inspecting. Diagnose a problem. Prescribe a solution. Monitor the implementation. Each one of the above could be at fault. So there's no time to relax.

WHAT WENT WRONG?[1]

FROM TIME TO TIME, everyone in life makes what we call a "mistake." This is a situation where what was expected either did not happen, or it happened with some undesired collateral damage.

How should one analyze a mistake? How should we go about answering the inevitable question: "What went wrong?"

It is in the nature of being human that we require an explanation for mistakes. Usually, we cannot rest until we have identified some attribution of causality. When none is readily available, we may suddenly become religious: "It's God's will." "The Devil made me do it." "It was not meant to be." And so on.

Those attributions are attractive because they are simple and easy to use. The only problem is that they do not allow us to learn from our mistakes.

Another easy-to-use attribution of causality is to personalize the cause. This process is known by many names, but is most memorably known as a witch-hunt. The idea is that you track down the troublemaker, the person responsible, and make sure he or she is easy to recognize. Notice that the troublemaker is objectified and dehumanized in this example.

Concluding that a specific person is culpable generally does not lead to anyone learning from the mistake—unless it just so happens that a) the problem is in fact this person's fault, which is not always the case; and b) the person who is supposed to learn can do so even though he or she has been objectified, which is even rarer.

How then is one to learn from mistakes so that they are not repeated?

1. Adizes Insights, July 2010.

First, one has to realize that every conscious action has two components: the making of the decision and the implementation of the decision. This leads to an important question: Was the decision wrong, or was the decision right and the implementation poor?

Let's begin with the first part of the question. What can be learned if the decision itself was wrong?

To make any headway here, we must move beyond simply being judgmental: "The good decision should have been..." We do not learn from judging. We learn by analyzing the process by which the wrong decision was made, so that the next time around we can follow a better process. Were the right people involved in making the decision? How did they go about deciding? Was there a constructive exchange of ideas before the decision was finalized? Was all the pertinent information considered? Were both the pros and cons of any alternative decision correctly valued? These questions are only a representative sample of the questions we must use to analyze the process by which the decision was made, but they will serve to give you a sense of the kind of analysis I am talking about.

Now let's move on to the second half of our question. Let's assume the decision was the appropriate one, and it is the implementation that needs reviewing.

In this, case, we should consider a different set of issues if we are to analyze and learn from the mistake. For instance: Which member of the team, if any, did not do what he or she was supposed to do? Why not? Was the timing off? Was the intensity of the task simply too high for the people responsible? Or, conversely, was the task perceived as too easy, and thus overlooked or minimized in importance?

It is imperative, in my view, to differentiate between errors in decision making and errors in implementation. They have totally different causes, and yield different lessons.

But what is the lesson to be learned if the analysis shows the decision was made well and the implementation was impeccable?

The lesson here is of humility: We are not in control of all variables that impact our life. In spite of doing our best, not everything works the way we want it to work. In this case, we learn to accept our limitations. We have to learn to surrender our ego; a lesson, it seems, that needs to be learned over and over throughout life.

Whose Problem Is It?[1]

To MANAGE WELL one needs to decide what to do and then implement that decision. To decide and not implement is useless. It's all talk and no action, a bunch of hot air that no one will take seriously. The flipside—to implement something that has not been decided—is also futile, with the added potential for being downright dangerous. There might be side effects that should have been considered when deciding.

Deciding and implementing are two sides of the same coin; one should not exist without the other. It follows then that those involved in implementation should be involved in the decision making. Many people make the mistake of separating the task of decision making from that of implementation. One person decides and someone else implements and the two don't talk to each other.

When diagnosing a problem and deciding what to do, bring into the discussion those who are needed for implementing the decision so that the details of implementation are discussed and paid attention to.

When you diagnose a problem ask yourself who is needed to solve it, to implement it.

To look at an example, let us assume that John Smith has not been performing well for a while. He is a problem. To implement a solution, his boss, David Johnson, is needed. That means to me that David is also the problem, not only John. Where was David all this time John was not performing? What is it David did not do that contributed to John's inadequate performance? Both are needed to diagnose the problem and both are needed to solve it.

1. Adizes Insights, September 2011.

When you diagnose a problem ask yourself who is needed to solve it, to implement it. Get them involved.

The above insight is very important for diagnosing and solving problems. Whoever has the authority to solve the problem is also part of the problem. And, those who are identified as the source of the problem, usually the subordinates, are necessary participants in the process of finding and implementing the solution.

The mistake I have noticed in my consulting practice is that there is a bifurcation: Management identifies the problem as being "them" and the solution is "us."

Wrong. If you are necessary for the solution, you are a source of the problem, too, and if you are causing the problem, you had better participate in finding the solution.

On Common Sense[1]

BRITISH AIRWAYS CLAIMS to have a first-class frequent travelers reward system. I flew with them for years. I have over 750,000 miles credit with them. And I am a very valuable client. I fly first class. Now, try to get a reward from BA. Useless. You have to spend hours waiting to get someone to talk to, and then the seats are not available on frequent travelers credit. Or if they are available, it is not on the dates you want to fly. And if it is available on the dates you want to fly, you have to fly via Timbuktu and wait there a day or two for a connection.

I gave up. I stopped flying British Airways, and still have unused frequent travelers points somewhere.

I switched to flying Lufthansa, thinking these Germans are good for their word. A promise is a promise. Once I got to the level of Senator in their program (I fly a lot), Lufthansa promised a whole slate of benefits. Almost a red carpet service. But when I tried to get a free ticket, I got the same lousy response I got from BA.

The best way to lose a customer forever is to overpromise and under-deliver.

How about Avis? Their slogan is "We try harder." Do they? Can management promise this and deliver it worldwide? I remember once getting a lousy service from a customer service person. Behind her on the wall was a big sign: "We try harder."

Does management believe that through advertising, through making promises, they can get us to buy and commit to their services? Or is it the actual service, even if not advertised, that makes the difference?

1.Adizes Insights, January 2013.

The best way to lose a customer forever is to overpromise and under-deliver. It is common sense.

I am standing in line to board a plane to Moscow. The line says priority lane for first class. My line to board is very long, almost as long as the line for economy. What is going on? Well, my lane is not only for first class, it is for business class, too. And for those with priority benefits from the frequent travelers program, and those who have a credit card from the airline, and who knows who else.

Why is this happening? One reason could be that the marketing department is not "connected" with the operations department. Those who make a promise have little, if anything, to do with those who deliver what is promised. Probably whoever was in charge of promoting the credit card thought it was a good idea to give card holders the benefit of priority boarding and did not consult those who are in charge of first class benefits.

In other words, disintegration.

This conclusion should not come as a surprise. At present, companies are very large and the task of managing them, coordinating all activities, promotions, etc., is overwhelming those who have to make decisions.

What is needed is group diagnosis of problems and open forums where problems are discussed and dealt with. Or maybe management has simply lost common sense. They rely on marketing gimmicks to produce results, forgetting that real service is what works, not marketing gimmicks.

Management is detached from the field, isolated in ivory tower executive offices, on the fortieth floor somewhere, reviewing tables and charts as if reviewing charts is the essence of their work rather than the service and quality of the products they provide. When was the last time your CEO called his or her own company and tried to buy something anonymously? There is much to learn from being a customer.

The biggest asset a manager can have in the complex world we live in is common sense. My suspicion is that many managers in the West have lost common sense. Maybe Ivan Ilich was right when he said education today is overeducating to the point that people lose common sense. Or maybe they watched too much television when they were growing up. Or smoked too much weed in college. Whatever it is, I sometimes scratch my head: Where has all the common sense gone?

The Fear of Success[1]

FEAR OF FAILURE is a well-known psychological concept. Some men and women, particularly in the arts, were gifted. Often extremely capable and talented. For a brief moment, they had the world at their feet. But then they began to turn their success, almost deliberately, into failure. They created art, but when it was time to exhibit they retreated, maybe even destroyed their art.

Why?

One explanation is that they were frightened of criticism, scared they would be judged a failure. And so, like a self-fulfilling prophecy, they failed by default by not performing or exhibiting.

I have come across a different pattern of behavior, of people who fear success.

A businessman I once knew invented a product that the market needed desperately. After an earthquake in Los Angeles, he came up with a new design for a fence that was flexible and pleasing to the eye. It could withstand any earthquake. And it was reasonably priced, cheaper than anything else on the market. It took off like wildfire. More demand than he could handle. Orders almost overwhelmed him. Did he celebrate by consolidating and expanding his product line? No. What he did instead was to start a fight with his partners and destroy the company he had built.

It was not the first time this had happened to him. He started very successful endeavors only to abandon them as they took off. In some strange way, he could not tolerate success. Failure was what he had learned to accommodate and expect. It was only by failing that he felt reassured.

1. Adizes Insights, October 2012.

You could say that succeeding toppled his sense of equilibrium, his comfort zone. It made him feel unstable.

Note that every animal has an environment where it feels most in its element. A swan would not like muddy water. Oxen on the other hand, prefer mud. Give them a green meadow and they will start digging till they create mud.

I believe it is the same with people. Some people feel comfortable with success and very uncomfortable with failure. They will work hard to turn a failure into success. And there are people who feel at home with failure and if by some miracle they succeed, they will work on turning the success into failure.

Such people always seem to find a way to fail even when the situation appears to lead to success.

Such people always seem to find a way to fail even when the situation appears to lead to success. Their unconscious takes over and they find a way to confirm what they already know: They are a failure.

This subject of being conditioned and then feeling most comfortable with that condition does not end only with fear of failure or fear of success. I know a man, a friend whom I am quite fond of, whose method of relating to someone is to start an argument. It is almost a reflex. I suspect that it is ruining his marriage. It is also mapping his face with real wrinkles even though he is still young and quite attractive. Yet he persists. Why? Because he is used to fighting. When anger takes hold I notice he feels in his element. It is, in a strange way, his comfort zone; the time when he feels natural and in control.

In the case of my friend, a loving, relaxed atmosphere has always bothered him. The moment a conversation takes that turn, he begins to feel uncomfortable. The way he has learned to self-soothe, to get over his discomfort, is to start an argument. That is his familiar territory and he knows best how to maneuver within it.

Where is the insight? We are managers. Leaders. Not therapists. We are not here to change people. We are here to lead them, capitalizing on the best they have to offer. Human resource development is not to change people, it is to enrich what they already are. Hire people who are used to success and are very uncomfortable with failure. The best is to find a person who had a major setback in his life and overcame it to make it a success nevertheless.

I am often asked to help change the style of a certain manager who is hostile to coworkers. He hates interactions, and prefers to work alone.

"Please change him," I am told. "You are the guru of change!" Sorry. It cannot be done. We can enrich a style. We cannot change a style.

Psychological theory tells us that personality cannot be changed. We are born with who we are. Many people do not accept this theory and valiantly try to change their subordinates or leaders. The sooner you learn to accept what is, the faster you can move to what should be.

How to Know Whom to Hire or Promote[1]

DURING MY FORTY YEARS OF CONSULTING, I have attended many meetings where the topic was who should be promoted to fill a vacant position. I've noticed that there is a pattern governing who might get promoted and who might get rejected for promotion.

A person often became a candidate for promotion or hiring based on his or her performance, or professional preparation and expertise; but that, in itself, did not secure the position. The question that usually determined whether a candidate got the position was whether their new subordinates would accept the new person as a leader.

I am currently consulting to a large real estate company. Because of the credit crisis, they are in dire need of a first-class CFO. One of the candidates had all the elements of a great resume: a degree from a leading business school; the right work experience, having worked for an even larger real estate development company; and he was willing to work for the salary my client was willing to pay. Yet he was not hired.

What was the problem? He was not hired because my client heard through the rumor mill that the guy was arrogant, fought with his colleagues, was not a team player, etc. None of this information is available in a resume. None of this will come up in an interview, either. Even if a previous employer is called for references, this information will not be provided because the candidate can sue the employer for defamation. One has to find the inside information somehow.

Are there any other factors that might impact someone's chances of getting promoted?

1. Adizes Insights, January 2012.

Yes there are. People are like trucks. When a truck gets overloaded with weight it starts to tremble; it does not move forward, just shakes in place. When a person is working beyond his capability he gets very nervous, easily upset, and has a short temper, as if saying, "I cannot take any more." A person working within his capability has a smile on his face and has a good sense of humor, as if saying, "You can put more responsibility on me."

Watch a candidate for a promotion. If she is nervous and easily upset, leave her where she is. She is not ready for promotion.

Another barrier for getting promoted is that the person is indispensable in his present position. Promoting him will create a problem; there is no one to fill the old shoes.

So, if you want to get promoted what should you do?

So, if you want to get promoted what should you do? Never stop learning, so your qualifications never became obsolete. Always get training beyond what your present task calls for.

And, never take on more than you can handle. Being a nice guy and sacrificing yourself for the sake of the company will not be rewarded with a promotion. You might get a one-time cash bonus, but in the long run you will be stymied.

Finally, make yourself dispensable. This might seem like the wrong strategy, because you are making yourself replaceable. But you can't be promoted unless someone can take your current place.

If you have developed beyond your present job, if your attitude is constructive and you appear positive and exciting, and if someone can fill your position, you are the prime candidate for the promotion you have been coveting.

"IF"[1]

IN MY CONSULTING EXPERIENCE I have come across many instances when people in the meeting say "*if* so and so happens, then…" I find this *if* to be disempowering. It does not point or direct us to think actively, proactively, about what we will do.

If sounds iffy. It gives me the feeling that the person speaking is not taking responsibility: "*If* it happens then we will see, who knows…"

Take a wallflower. She has no dates. She is lonely. She might say, "*If* someone asks me out *then* I will…"

If does not built hope. It gives control to the outside world, to external forces. We have nothing to do, just wait.

Instead of using *if*, I request that my clients use the word *when*.

"*When* I am asked out I will…"

Can you feel that this second sentence has hope in it, that it empowers?

This is especially important for bureaucratic organizations when they discuss competition. "*If* competition increases its pressure then we should…" Now use the word *when*: "*When* competition increases its pressure we need to…" The word *when* is already one of the four imperatives of decision making. When you use the word *when* you are already planning to do something. *When* feels much more threatening and thus the probability of the company getting off its seat and starting to do something is much higher.

Words are not just words. They evoke maps in our consciousness and cause behavior. We have to be careful which words we chose and pay attention to whether they generate the behavior we want or not.

1. Adizes Insights, January 2014.

PART III

�֍

MANAGING CHANGE

Change and Its Repercussions for Leadership[1]

WHILE CHANGE HAS BEEN EVER-PRESENT for millions of years, today it has taken on a role in our lives that is far more formidable, and even dangerous. We now tend to find ourselves at a loss, unable to respond to change adequately or within a necessary time frame. In short, we are overwhelmed.

Partly, this is because the nature of change has taken on a different face. It has been affected drastically and irreversibly by three factors: speed, frequency, and interdependence.

Let me start with speed. Change keeps accelerating with a kind of continuous velocity that makes it difficult to pause so that we can adapt and adjust to, let alone embrace, the rapid new forces that have come to define us and our society. It is different from earlier forms of change, not only in terms of frequency and rapidity, but in its very nature. It is multi-faceted, multi-disciplinary, and very much interconnected. All macro subsystems suddenly seem to overlap, from technology to economics and politics to the socio-cultural environment. And change in one sector of our society delivers repercussions that are felt in other areas within a very short period of time.

Take the internet, a technological innovation which has changed the nature of retailing (an economic impact), of education (a social impact), and of information sharing, which has mobilized people to change governments (a political impact).

This high velocity and interdependence leads to a world that is increasingly complex, with accompanying problems that are exceedingly difficult to solve. The solutions themselves require approaches simultaneously

1. Presentation made at the World Economic Forum, Davos, Switzerland, January 24, 2014.

applied by people from different disciplines. Nor is that always sufficient. Timing is often of essence when making a decision today, because by the time a solution is at hand, ready for implementation, the environment has already changed. Many of the facts (and situations) have become outdated or irrelevant.

When change occurs we need to make a decision. Often quickly. What shall we do about the "new event" that was caused by change? Since it is new, there is, by definition, uncertainty confronting the decision maker. The decision made needs to be implemented and that means undertaking risk. It might work. It might not. In this new complex environment, then, uncertainty and risk are heightened significantly. They have caused the demise of many corporations. Corporate leaders, deprived of what they consider sufficient advance notice, have suddenly found themselves awash in trouble faster than anything they experienced in the past.

The same pattern applies to nation states. I leave you to fill in the names of countries.

The result is that CEOs and heads of state alike are faced with totally new forms of complexity without past experience to guide them.

The latest American financial crisis is a case in point. The crisis came as a surprise. No one expected it. Not the Department of Treasury, nor the president's Council of Economic Advisors, nor the Federal Reserve. The US federal government was forced to change its policies every few days. Why? Because it did not have a clear road map or understanding of the complexity of the situation. There was no ready solution, or even a formula at hand. It soon became clear that economic answers to the problem had unfortunate political and social repercussions. A solution that was palatable economically was viewed as impractical, if not unworkable, because it had political repercussions.

It should be noted that the problems confronting the European Union are even more complex inasmuch as they concern multiple nations, each with a different form of governance set of national interests, separate national culture, and its own cycles of change. Each nation is coping separately with an economic crisis that, in practical terms, ties them all together.

Is there a way to decrease the uncertainty and risk?

From my experience of over forty years in consulting to corporations and leaders of countries, I would say, emphatically, yes, there is.

On the corporate level, the starting point requires a new way of thinking, particularly with respect to organizations and the structure of leadership. Traditionally corporations structure their organization around a single leader. But rather than a single voice, today's complexity requires a complementary team of managers and collaborative leadership, joined together to find solutions to problems that can quickly cause a company to go under. This is really a profound change in our present day construct of leadership, and its importance cannot be overemphasized. It involves composing a team of creative entrepreneurs, risk-averse professionals, and task-oriented technocrats who are cognizant of the importance of making and implementing decisions in a timely fashion, and of working collaboratively to arrive at a solution.

On the corporate level, the starting point requires a new way of thinking.

Why a complementary team? Because their different styles and different judgments cross-pollinate one another. They begin with different ways of knowing and understanding, and, by complementing one another, they reduce the degree of uncertainty. In the end, they improve the quality of the decision itself.

Compare that to a decision rendered by, say, a single entrepreneur presiding over a task force under his command. The entrepreneur will probably make a decision with less information than a risk-averse professional requires. On the other hand, if the corporate leader is himself a risk-averse specialist making the decision alone, he will take longer to decide… and the timing of the decision will likely be flawed.

In brief, complementary teams turn out to be far more effective than individual leaders in leading corporations in times of complex change.

Now, what is needed to reduce risk?

Usually multiple groups, within a government or a corporation, are necessary for efficient, timely implementation of a decision. The problem is that each group has its own interests. If the interests collide and there actually is no common interest, the probability that the decision will be implemented correctly is drastically reduced. The greater the degree of diversity in interests among the necessary groups, the more difficult the implementation of a solution.

Let me restate: Making effective policy decisions in a chronic, accelerated, complex, changing environment requires complementary, collaborative leadership. Leaders, in turn, need to be capable of building coalitions to secure common interests among the parties necessary for efficient implementation.

The above factors are necessary, but not sufficient, since they carry a burden: On a corporate level, a team of leaders with different styles seeking a common interest inevitably means that there will be conflict. From experience we know it is bound to happen among the interested parties, in part because of their different styles. On a macro or nation-state level, there will be conflict too: Opposing political parties do not necessarily collaborate constructively. We recognize this in the acrimonious relationships between Democrats and Republicans in the United States. Their actions hamper the government's ability to function. In addition, the nation's interest groups—in the US, for example, the military industrial complex, in other countries, the trade unions—make it extremely difficult to reach common agreement on interests and needs. See: France, Greece, and Spain.

How to make it work?

This is going to sound over-simplified. It is not. Far, far from it. I have devoted over forty years of my professional life to studying what works when it comes to managing change effectively and efficiently, within corporations as well as governments. It is not a simple concept. It is simplified so it can be implemented. It has been tested successfully within hundreds of corporations worldwide and, to a lesser degree, within governments.

What is required at this point within the complementary team, up and down the corporate and political ladder, is *mutual respect*. Respect, as Emanuel Kant said, means to recognize the sovereignty of the other party to think differently. When there is mutual respect there is a willingness to learn from each other. There is a greater tolerance for differences in opinion. Without arguments and collaboration shaped and governed by respect, a faulty and wrong decision will emerge and lots of energy will be wasted; or—just as harmful—decisions will be deferred, bringing corporate or national progress to a halt. Just like the latest budget debate in the American congress.

To deal with the conflicts, which can be destructive when multiple interests are involved, is a bit more difficult. Mutual respect is not enough. Here we also need mutual trust.

Trust means that if I yield my interest now for the benefit of another group, in time I will be rewarded. It is based on a belief in a "growing pie," that there is enough for everyone and giving up now on some point is worth doing because it will help the pie grow, and eventually there will be more for me too.

When there is trust there is collaboration. Decisions are implemented in the spirit in which they were made, and the risk is thus lower. When there is an absence of trust, collaboration ceases and decisions are made in the context of a different frame of reference, which unfortunately only increases the risk.

It bears repeating: Mutual trust and respect reduce uncertainty and risk in decision making and implementation.

What is the role of leadership then? To develop and nurture a culture of mutual trust and respect within the system, be it a corporation or a government.

Look at the world around us. What does Switzerland have in terms of natural resources? Or Japan? Practically nothing. Nevertheless, both countries by and large have enjoyed economic success. On the other hand, take South Africa. It has enormous resources in gold and diamonds, but its economic success is limited at best. What is the difference? The culture.

When there is MT&R, there is cooperation and collaboration and the system not only survives, but prospers at all levels, whether it is a family, a corporation, or a nation.

I was asked recently by several government leaders for a proposed solution to the latest economic crisis. My answer was, whatever you do, do not lose the trust and respect of the nation's people. I believe that trust and respect are the most important assets a government, indeed a system on any level, can possess. They are the most difficult to develop, and the easiest to lose.

The reality is that trust and respect are threatened by change. Why? Because change increases uncertainty and risk, and thereby tests our trust and our respect for one another.

It appears that politicians in general are losing the respect and the trust of the populace. Worldwide. I attribute this to the rapid rate of change, which politicians have deep trouble responding to with any success. It is a constant struggle. The problems keep getting more complex every day, and politicians' popularity keeps getting lower, falling day by day. The repercussions can be catastrophic: not just loss of power for the leaders, but loss of power for the state as well.

It is probably a truism by now: The greater the rate of change the more acute the conflicts. In the twentieth century more people were murdered than in the entire history of mankind. What will the twenty-first century bring, with the proliferation of nuclear weapons and weapons of mass destruction?

We should ask ourselves whether the world is marching to its destruction or to the Age of Aquarius. I suggest that it depends upon whether MT&R among nations, people, and religions will be the guiding compass or not.

A related conundrum confronts us on the corporate level. Which corporations will succeed and which will go under? Again, I would say that it depends whether MT&R can help solve differences between management, workers, and stockholders, and whether a unity of interests can be produced. One factor that made Germany successful in recent decades was the collaboration of management and workers through the system of co-determination.

The more collaboration the better in time of change.

It is important to recognize these realities. Change is a centripetal force. Technology has brought the world closer together. But without MT&R, change becomes a centrifugal force, too.

Today the conflicts between political parties are particularly bitter. Conflicts of interests increasingly drive people and political parties further and further apart, without much hope of a collaborative solution. Trust is rapidly disappearing. And disintegration within corporations, the silo phenomenon, is a repetitive syndrome.

Political leaders in democratic society have, for the most part, become prisoners of the polls. They find themselves constrained, unable to take positions that they recognize are necessary for the health of the economy. The pressure groups within the society are too vocal, and our new social media galvanizes the voters to respond immediately and emotionally to the latest pressure. (See Greece and France.)

In the face of this broad-ranging decline, destructive conflicts have begun to assume a dominating role, which, in turn, appears to be opening the door to totalitarian leadership.

What is the solution?

The democratic system designed hundreds of years ago does not seem to be responding well anymore to the challenge that chronic and complex change poses. The remedy on the macro level is to reconsider how democracy should work, given the chaotic environment we live in. It needs to be reconstructed. The restructuring begins with developing paths towards mutual respect and trust. It will require structural and educational changes that will mean a paradigmatic shift in our value system.

On the corporate level, with respect to leadership, education, and training, business schools need to redesign their curricula to move away from concentrating on individual leadership and begin to emphasize the necessity of collaborative management and teamwork. The curricula must begin to focus on ways to construct coalitions whose main goal is to achieve common interests.

Major changes in our environment call for major changes in how we manage.

LEADING CHANGE FOR SUSTAINABLE INNOVATION[1]

EACH WORD IN THE TITLE ABOVE is very popular today. It has become a fad at management retreats to discuss the concepts of leadership, sustainability, change, and innovation. But is this what is really important?

Let us discuss.

In a company that produces oral-hygiene products, a young business school graduate is hired. Eager to prove his worth, he comes up with a recommendation for management on how to increase profitability. His recommendation is to enlarge the hole in the toothpaste tube, so that with the same squeeze, consumers will get more toothpaste out of the tube. It is expected this would increase the consumption of toothpaste by 100%. Since the marginal increase in costs of making a bigger hole in the tube is close to nothing, the increase in revenues will correspond to an almost 100% increase in profits. What a great idea. What a genius. The kid gets a promotion and a bonus.

Now, is this truly an innovation? I think so.

Is it sustainable? Why not? It produces profits, and most consumers probably do not notice that their toothpaste gets used up faster than usual. Even if they do notice, they probably blame themselves for squeezing the tube too hard.

Does the young man's innovation qualify as leadership? It will probably be considered as such. The kid stood out in the crowd and produced profitable change in the company.

It was sustainable. It was leadership. It was innovation. It was profitable.

1. Adizes Insights, September 2011.

Is this what we should do as managers, as business leaders?

I ask you.

Now, let us take another example. There is a health center in California that promotes a vegan diet. (This, like the previous anecdote, is a true story.) At this health center, the doctors try to change our habit of eating animal products, oil, salt, sugar, and processed food, to instead eat what our ancestors in the Stone Age ate: vegetables, fruits, legumes, rice and beans...a plant-based diet.

What should be the goal?

Would this be considered an innovation? I do not think so. Not for taking us back 2,000 years.

Is it sustainable? Probably not. One of the goals of this vegan diet is to lose weight.

Nor does the center make a large profit. How many people do you think will pay a large amount of money to go there and eat vegetables and fruit all day long? There is no money in this business. If there were, hundreds of centers like it would open up all over the place, like mushrooms after the rain. But look at how quickly a chain of outlets selling cupcakes expands, or a chain that sells fried food. That is how you make money: You sell what people want to buy. You innovate something the market approves of.

But is this the right thing to do?

The toothpaste company is making more money, all right, but it is also wasting resources. Is that good for society? The vegetarian center is making very marginal profits while struggling to heal people of obesity and the diseases that accompany it, such as diabetes, heart attacks, strokes, lupus, and other inflammations. Is that good for society, even though the center is not making good money?

Making money should not be the goal. Innovation should not be the goal. Sustainability should not be the goal. Even leadership should not be the goal. They are all means to achieve the real goal.

What should be the goal?

Sociologists tell us that the purpose of both humans and organizations is survival. But look at how we eat. Look at how we treat our air, water, and earth. Look at the crime rate. Look at how many children murder their parents—something unheard of in primitive society. And what about the nuclear devices we developed, which can destroy society and the world as we know it?

Are we doing what it takes to survive, or are we slowly but surely moving toward the destruction of civilization? The goal of survivability is a "should" goal, but it does not appear to be the goal we actually aim for in our behavior as a society.

The medical profession says the goal of the human organism is to reproduce itself; we are reproductive machines. That sounds to me like another way of saying survival of the species, a goal that is slightly wider than the one sociology offers us. But are we doing what it takes to prolong the life of our species? Are we leaving a better world than the world our parents gave us?

Technology-wise, yes. We definitely have it better than our ancestors. Medicine has advanced beyond what our grandparents could even dream about. But is it a better world?

I suggest that it is not.

Overall, we are destroying the world we live in: polluting the air, the water, and the earth. Our children will have to go to a zoo to see animals we see all around us today. Our grandchildren will never see some of the flowers whose scents we appreciate today, because they are becoming extinct right now—this moment, as we speak. They will never see certain species of fish and birds. Because of air pollution, they will never be awed by the magnificent spectacle of a clear sunset.

What are we doing? What should be the goal?

Tikun olam. That should be the goal. *Tikun olam* is the ancient Hebrew explanation for why we are here on this planet. The literal translation is "to repair the world," in other words, to leave it a better world when we die than how we found it when we were born.

Why "to repair?" Because of entropy. Because of change. The world is constantly changing, but not for the better—unless we take the initiative and proactively make change for the better. Our garden will become a messy jungle of weeds unless we tend it. Our car will fall apart unless it is maintained. Our marriage will lose its creative intimacy if we ignore its demands.

We have to work the garden. Repair the car. Invest time in our marriage. Work on our community. Work for our country. Help heal the earth.

Yes, *tikun olam* means to heal the world, to leave it a better place than the one we inherited.

Innovation, sustainability, and leadership are needed, but they must be viewed through the following prism: Does our innovation heal the world, or does it damage the world?

All our actions should have a spiritual criterion. Profits should not be the goal. They should be the constraint: Of course we do not want to go bankrupt, but the goal should be to make a better world. The benefit must be higher than the cost—and I'm talking about the cost not just to a company but also to the world, to society, to our children.

I read somewhere that it is not true we are passing on the world to our children. In fact, we are borrowing the world from our children. We are leaving them with a deficit they might not be able to pay; leaving them a dirty, messy world that they will have to clean up in order to survive.

And all this is coming from a single erroneous, misguided concept of profit as a goal.

Innovation, yes—but for what?

Sustainability, yes—but for what?

Leadership, sure—but for what?

Profit, yes—but at what cost?

Let us not forget what we are really in this world for. Let us not forget that as children of God, we are here to serve love and not hate, to serve the good of the world, because our days are numbered and we cannot take anything with us.

What counts is not what we take, but what we leave behind.

ORDERS OF CHANGE[1]

PAUL WATZLAWICK, IN HIS BOOK *CHANGE,* coined the concept of "orders of change."

He described three orders that are distinguished by the depth of the change intended.

I differentiate the orders of change with PAEI. (Not strange, is it?)

Change order number 1 is (P): change *what* you are doing without changing the how, the why, or the who.

Change order number 2 is (A): change *how* you are doing whatever you are doing, but not the why nor the who.

> *How deep should a change be in an organization?*

Change order 3 is (E): change *why* you are doing what and how you are doing.

Change number 4 is the deepest change, (I): it is to change *who* you are; change your values. It drives new whys, new whats, and new hows.

How deep should a change be in an organization?

I find a typical mistake is to change only *what* we do and then be surprised that the change is superficial and not sustainable.

As an example, consider someone who needs to lose weight. Change order number 1 is to change what you eat; eat fewer calories. How many of you have counted calories and eventually got tired of the futility of the experiment and stopped the diet?

Change number 2: Change *how you eat.* Eat slowly. Eat many meals a day,

1. Adizes Insights, March 2012.

each with small portions. When you eat, eat consciously. Do not read the newspaper. Do not watch TV. Chew a lot, etc.

Have you tried those types of diets? How has it worked for you?

Now consider an (E) change, change number 3. That is where psychologists try to help you to lose weight: "*Why* are you overeating?" "What benefits do you get from overeating?" And how does that work?

My understanding is that over ninety percent of those trying to diet fail over time (and that includes me).

Why?

Because the depth of the change necessary to lose weight sustainably is much deeper than 3. You have to change the (I): *who* you are, how you perceive yourself; you have to change your self-image.

You have to start loving being skinny rather than hating being fat.

In diagnosing a problem you have to ask yourself what degree of change is necessary in order to solve this problem sustainably. Sustainably does not mean forever. Nothing is forever. It should be long enough to conclude that you have gained control over the problem.

Control does not mean never failing to stay on course. It means you have developed the capability to promptly make a corrective action so the deviation is not prolonged or permanent.

THE PROBLEM-SOLVING CYCLE: WHAT COULD GO WRONG?[1]

IN ORDER TO SOLVE A PROBLEM we must first be aware that there is a problem. In order to be aware one has to define what is it that one should be aware of. A problem is a result or a process that is unexpected and/or undesirable. There are many examples to manifest this definition: undesirable and unexpected. For example, you lost money in a business when you did not expect to lose money. It was clearly not desirable.

An expected undesirable example would be when you know you are in a bad partnership that is going to be trouble and you nevertheless do not act on it promptly.

A third situation, which is desirable but unexpected, is also a problem: You made more money than you expected; it was luck and luck cannot be repeated or reproduced. So, your rejoicing is misplaced. It might make you complacent with dire consequences in a changing environment.

If you are not aware that there is a problem, obviously you are not going to act to solve it. Thus, awareness is the precondition to solving problems.

Being aware, however, is not enough. One has to be conscious of the problem. Conscious means to realize the repercussions of not solving the problem.

Many people realize—are aware—that they are eating junk food. But they are not conscious of the repercussions of eating junk food. The repercussions are in the long run and there is always the hope that "it will not hurt me; the repercussions do not apply to me."

Being conscious is not enough for solving a problem either. One needs to

1. Adizes Insights, June 2011.

diagnose the problem. For that, one has to accumulate the appropriate information. With bad information there will most probably be a bad diagnosis.

Assume you are aware that the market is changing. It is undesirable but expected. You are conscious that if you do not change the business model you are using you might lose your market and business, and the repercussions could be dire.

Now what?

> ### *Knowing the problem does not mean you have the right solution.*

You have to diagnose what the problem is: how is the market changing, how will it impact your company, etc. You have to accumulate information. The next step is to diagnose that information.

It is possible to fail this step: You could have accumulated the wrong information, which gave you the wrong diagnosis; or got the right information but made the wrong diagnosis.

Let us now say that you were aware that there is a problem, you were conscious of the repercussions, you got the right information, and you reached the most adequate diagnosis. Now what?

Knowing the problem, that is, having the right diagnosis, does not mean you have the right solution. Even some medical doctors fail here: They diagnose the right illness but prescribe the wrong medicine.

Now let us assume that the prescription, the solution, was right. Does it mean we are done? We diagnosed the problem and solved it. What else is there?

Guess what? One needs to implement the solution. How many people do you know who are aware of being overweight, are conscious that it will cause high blood pressure and diabetes, have diagnosed their problem and concluded that they are eating the wrong food. They know what their diet should be—they have the solution in their hand. But notice: They are not acting on the solution. They are not implementing it.

So let us assume that the person does implement the solution. Are we done now? No!

Here is an example: One is aware of being overweight. It is easy to be aware of this problem, just get on the scale.

Conscious: yes. The blood pressure and cholesterol are unacceptably high and you are conscious that it can lead to a heart attack.

The diagnosis: You are eating junk food.

Solution: Get on a diet. When you monitor the implementation of your decision you realize that the implementation is not working well. You depart from the diet frequently. So when monitoring you realize you still have the problem.

So start again: The problem is not the junk food. The problem is you. You are addicted to salt and sugar and fatty food.

The solution was wrong because it addressed the wrong problem: junk food. What is needed is a solution that addresses the right problem: addiction to salt, sugar, and fat. Going on a diet does not solve an addiction problem. You need a totally different solution, and if that one does not work either, start the process again and again and again, until the problem disappears.

We can fail in solving a problem along this arduous road: We were not aware there was a problem until it became a crisis. Or, we were aware but neglected to do anything because we were not conscious of its repercussions. Or, we were conscious but we got the wrong data and thus the wrong diagnosis. Or, the data was right but the diagnosis was bad. Or, the diagnosis was right but the prescription, the solution was wrong. Or, everything up to this point was right—the diagnosis and the solution—but the implementation was bad. Or, the last mistake, everything was right—we were aware, conscious, got the right data, discovered the right diagnosis, and the right solution, and implemented it—but we did not monitor how is the implemented solution working.

Look at what good surgeons do: After the surgery, which is the solution to the problem, they call you and ask you how are you doing. They do post-surgery monitoring even though they believe they performed a good surgery. One never knows for sure until the solution actually works.

Problem solving is not as easy as defining your problem and solving it. It is a complicated string of steps that need to be taken, and along the way many mistakes can be made.

What I hope this insight provides is a map to analyze which step was not done well so your problem can be solved.

The Voice of the Consumer: Does Everyone Hear It?[1]

MARKETING GURUS almost always insist that organizations listen to the voices of their customers. It is critical for the company to do so, but the question is how?

Think of your organization as a living organism. You cannot have only the "skin" of the organization, the client interface—the marketing department, the sales department, or the help desk—be the only part of the body that hears what the client has to say. If information from the customer never penetrates to any other part of the organization, the company will be unable to respond effectively.

So the question is how to make the customer's voice heard throughout the entire organization, so that the company can satisfy those customers' expectations.

Everything has a reason for being

The answer, I believe, lies in changing the internal dynamic of the organization. Every unit in the organization should have a client. Customers are the client of the sales department and sales is the client of the production department. Accounting has everyone in the organization as its clients. Each unit should be listening to the voice of their clients. Usually, when we use the word "customer" we are referring only to the sales or marketing department, which implies that those departments are the only ones that are obliged to listen. I emphasize the term "client" to make the point that *all* parts of the organization must serve *somebody*. The interdependence of all parts has to be recognized. If each unit serves its clients well it will be easier to satisfy the ultimate client needs, i.e., those

1. Adizes Insights, February 2011.

of the customer. The right products will be delivered at the right time at the right price, etc. No single part of the organization, alone, can satisfy all of the commitments that an entire organization exists to fulfill.

Look at any organism. Each part of the body exists in order to serve some other part. The heart has a client: Its client is the rest of the body, and the service it performs for that client is to circulate the blood. The lungs have a client: They send oxygen to the bloodstream. The only entity in the body that doesn't have a client, and serves only itself, is a cancer.

How do businesses measure whether they are satisfying their customers?

Organizational cancers are people or departments that serve no one but themselves. An organizational cancer arises when a person, a unit, or a work group, says, in effect:

- We don't know who our clients are, so how can we serve them? or,

- We know who our clients are, but we do not know their needs (we've never asked); or,

- We serve, but we do so on our own terms.

An organizational cancer can impede healthy growth and adaptation, and even bring the enterprise to its demise.

Every manager, every employee, every unit of the organization, large or small, should have a client to serve. If everyone in the organization serves his clients well, then the customer's voice will be heard, and his needs will eventually be served.

Take the following chain for an illustration: Sales listens to the customer, then passes the information it receives to marketing, which listens attentively, because the sales department is one of its clients. After analyzing the information, marketing adds its own recommendations and passes it to another of its clients: new product development or improvement engineering. Those departments serve production, which is a client of the supply chain department.

As can be seen from this illustration, if all departments are listening to their clients, eventually the customer's voice will not only be heard but will be listened to and acted upon.

How do businesses measure whether they are satisfying their customers? They measure revenues—repeat sales. But how do you measure the success of departments that have *internal* clients, that do not actually *buy* goods and services? Thus there are no sales by which to gauge the success of the unit. What to do? To find out whether that unit is effective, you must ask yourself: "If this unit's clients had a choice, would they come back?"

Be honest in your evaluation. Or even better, ask the internal clients themselves to give you an honest answer.

THE COURAGE TO CHANGE[1]

W HY IS COURAGE NEEDED in leading change? To answer this question I need to first address the theme of this celebration: "Creating the Future."

Ladies and gentlemen, the title is wrong. You cannot create the future. The title is missing one word, a *critical* word, which would make it right.

The human mind responds to thoughts literally, not unlike a computer: You cannot type a certain instruction into your computer and expect it to deliver different information than what you asked it to do. Our mind works the same way. It handles thoughts literally. If you make the decision "I will go on a diet tomorrow," when you wake up the next morning your mind will ask you: Is today tomorrow? Since the answer is obviously "no," you probably will not start your diet.

You cannot create the future. Like the past, which once existed but no longer does, the future does not exist either. What exists in reality—and the *only* thing that exists—is what you are creating *now*.

This concept, that the only thing that is real is now, has important implications for the task of planning. Planning is not deciding what we will do tomorrow. Effective planning is deciding what we are going to do *right* now in order to prepare for tomorrow.

Thus, the theme for this celebration should have been: "Creating *for* the Future."

But that begs the question: If one needs to create the future now, how does one know what to do now? For that we need to be creative, be willing to take risks, and, as the title for this presentation says, have courage.

1. Keynote presentation celebrating the twenty-fifth anniversary of IEDC, Bled School of Management, Bled, Slovenia, October 14, 2011.

First, why creativity?

Creativity is necessary precisely because we need to act now in anticipation of the future, when no one can tell for sure what it will be. We must imagine the future. We must build scenarios. We must use our creativity to recognize a pattern and fill in the missing pieces in order to get the total picture. In other words, we should handle uncertainty with creativity.

Now, why willingness to take risks?

Because in order to create *for* the future, which is uncertain, we need to act in the present, and that is risky. Maybe the future we imagined and acted in anticipation of will not happen. All our preparations in the present may turn out to be a waste of energy, effort, and resources. Maybe we were wrong, and usually there is a price to be paid for being wrong.

> *Now, why willingness to take risks?*

Being proactive in a situation that has not occurred yet, we run the risk of being criticized and even ridiculed.

Philosophically speaking, there is no present. The present is a split second between the past and the future. It either happened already or is going to happen. For some people, usually the ones with a conservative outlook, the present is a continuation of the past. For people who are creative, willing to take risks, and have the courage to act—the liberals—it is the beginning of the future.

Those who continue living in the past can neither understand nor appreciate people who are, in the present, preparing for a future that has not happened yet. To act today in anticipation of the future, leaders of change must have courage to take risks and withstand the criticism and ridicule of those who are stuck in the past.

That is why they are called leaders, not followers.

International Executive Development Center, the institution celebrating its twenty-fifth anniversary today, epitomized the courage to change. It did so it in the past. And it is doing so now.

How?

Allow me to analyze the past first. Twenty-five years ago, Professor Danica Purg had the courage to establish—singlehandedly!—the IEDC in a country where the curriculum of executive education had historically been determined by Marxist ideology, a country that was just beginning the struggle to introduce market forces as regulators of economic behavior. This called for a significant paradigm shift in thinking. It required courage to take on the establishment. And she succeeded not only in developing Slovenian executives, but also in establishing an organization that transcended the borders of Slovenia, her home country, to serve the entire Central and Eastern blocs in their parallel struggles to transform themselves. Her efforts ultimately had an impact even beyond Central and Eastern Europe, inspiring changes in executive education as taught today in Western Europe and Asia. In 2010, Professor Purg was voted Dean of the Year by the Academy of International Business, a leading organization of scholars and specialists in her field. No surprise there.

Now, how about having courage to lead change at the present time?

Ladies and gentlemen, something very significant is happening at present that is imposing new demands on executive leadership. Creativity, risk taking, and courage are not enough anymore.

I suggest to you that business leadership is not what developed countries need the most now. Developed countries are already saturated with things. The creating, manufacturing, and selling of things that improve our standard of living are reducing our quality of life. Because we are destroying the environment.

Change is accelerating in modern society, and different macro subsystems advance and change at different speeds. Technology is changing the fastest (thus increasing our standard of living) while social values are changing the slowest. This disparity in speeds of change creates gaps, manifested by rising systemic social problems that are increasing in their severity, like crime, unemployment, social unrest, socio-political alienation, and other manifestations of a deteriorating quality of life.

As you see, a higher standard of living does not necessarily bring a higher quality of life. I suggest to you that just the opposite is the truth.

What developed countries need now more than ever are *social* leaders, what Andre Malraux, France's first minister of culture, once called social animators: People who identify society's developing cultural and social needs and trends, people who are able to mobilize resources and social forces in the present to create for a better future.

But how does one go about becoming a social leader? How does one deal with those systemic socio-economic problems?

What must come into play to be a social leader is not just creativity, risk taking, and courage, like in the past, but *values*: the ability to distinguish between right and wrong. Modern society, in order to create a better future today, needs leaders who are capable of making value choices.

How does anyone arrive at such values? Not by using logic or mathematical cost-value relationships, but by listening to one's heart. That is what makes us human, what differentiates us from animals. True social leaders, those who can lead us to a better future, think not only with their heads but also with their hearts.

It is infinitely more difficult to teach values than to teach facts and formulas. To be human it is not enough to be born in a human body. I believe this aspect of leadership development, to think with one's heart and not only with one's head, is missing altogether in today's executive leadership development programs.

Here again, Professor Purg, the founder and indisputable leader of the IEDC, has shown courage and provided leadership in bringing values, experientially, into executive leadership development.

For example, she developed a program for executives from Britain to visit Bosnia to study management principles, but also to meet the victims of the ferocious war there and see for themselves what happens—to mothers, to children, to the elderly—when modern military technology is combined with the values of the Stone Age. By the end of the program, some executives were weeping.

Executive development should not only be to open people's minds, but also to open people's hearts to feel.

Society needs to create today the leaders of tomorrow—a new breed of leaders whose social values drive their materialistic decisions, rather than leaders who, driven by materialistic goals, compromise social values.

We need leaders who have the courage to change society driven by materialism to a society driven by values. And here, Professor Purg had the courage to change leadership development once again.

I feel privileged to be associated with IEDC, a school with a view, literally as well as metaphorically, and applaud the leadership of Professor Purg, and may I wish that she celebrates the fiftieth anniversary of this school in good health and with the same energy courage requires.

Profits and Prostitution[1]

I N MY LECTURES I say that the focus of an organization should not be profits. Profits are like the scoreboard of a tennis match. The focus should be on playing well. If you play better than the competition, you will win. For organizations, the focus should be on being healthier than the competition. The reward for being healthy is profits.

Being a healthy organization means that all four roles of PAEI are fulfilled: The company is satisfying present client needs (P); is doing so efficiently (A); is proactive to deal with anticipated changes (E); and is organically interdependent, with transparency and functional flow of energy between the parts that comprise the organization which enables collaboration (no silos) (I).

Profits in the short and long run are the product of being healthy, of having a PAEI organization.

Satisfying client needs, (P), brings revenues. Satisfying those needs at a lower cost (i.e., efficiently) than the price clients are willing to pay to satisfy their needs, (A), produces profits in the short run. Being proactive, (E), and organic, (I), make the organization effective and efficient in the long run, and that will make it profitable in the long run, too.

Conclusion: The goal of organizations should be to achieve and maintain their health. If they do, the reward is profits.

It reminds me of sex: Like sex, profits should be the *result* of healthy organizational relationships, not the purpose of the relationship. For whom is sex the purpose of the relationship? For prostitutes. It is money that drives their behavior. Relationships are non-existent.

That brings me to the insight: Business people who focus on profit as a goal, rather than the health of the organization, are prostituting themselves.

1. Adizes Insights, March 2012.

Developing Future Leaders[1]

W E HAVE THREE WORDS in our topic: *developing*, *future*, and *leaders*. Let me first talk about the future, then about what it means to be a leader in the future. Finally, I will address the issue of leadership development.

I have been in the field of change management for forty years, and I have come to a very sad conclusion: You should not try to predict the future. Although there are twenty Nobel Prize winners in economics in the United States, none of them managed to predict the economic crisis from which we are emerging just now. Who would have believed that Lehman Brothers would go broke? Who would have believed that if the US government had not helped the country's banks they would have all gone bankrupt?

Remember how arrogant General Motors used to be, saying that what is good for General Motors is good for America. That company would have also gone down the drain without the support of the US government. Nobody predicted that.

Why are we unable to predict the future? Because the world has become extremely complex. It is not atomistic anymore. Its different parts are all interconnected and overlapping. Technology advances have sizable social repercussions, which in turn have political and economic repercussions. It is one big bouillabaisse.

Is it not strange that nobody went to prison for the financial crisis? Do you know why? Because nobody can figure out who is the culprit. Even the government did not know what to do. They were changing their policies every twenty-four hours: "Let's do this! No, wait; let us do that. No,

---

1. Keynote presentation at the Central and Eastern European Management Development Association's twentieth anniversary, under the auspices of the United Nations. Delivered on September 25, 2013 in Bled, Slovenia.

no, that is not a good idea. Let us do something else." Why was that? Because they did not know what to do. Even the Federal Reserve admitted that the crisis was unpredictable and had no prepared solution.

We are becoming increasingly confused. Do we really know what is going on?

Moreover because of accelerated change we are becoming older at a younger age. Some people are old at the age of forty. They are considered too old to be given a job. They are too old for the new technologies that are in vogue. I am ready to bet that the age at which people are considered old is going to fall even further. In some fields, like rock music, you are too old at twenty-three.

What are we supposed to do?

Two things to start with:

First, you cannot be educated in one particular field and assume that this will be enough for the future. You have to have a multidisciplinary education. That is why I told the International Academy of Management that our business education is wrong. We teach marketing, finance, sales, supply chains, human resources, and accounting, and we assume that we can manage the totality. But there is no course that teaches anything about the totality. How do you integrate all elements of the system? How do you think in a systemic, integrated way?

Business education should have a much wider scope. It should provide a background in political science and sociology, among other fields. You have to know multiple disciplines so that you are not lost in one.

Training of future leaders has to be systemic. At the Adizes Graduate School, the most important courses for future leaders are not finance, strategic planning, or human resources. They are epistemology and systemic thinking. Epistemology has to do with knowing what you know.

Second, please, do not ever graduate. The diploma that you get from the Adizes Graduate School does not say that so-and-so completed his studies. A good diploma should say the graduate is "allowed to continue studying." The day you stop learning, you stop changing, and unless you change, you die slowly. This happens to people, companies, cities, and countries. The world is changing so fast that you should never assume that you know enough. As you study, you should not only discover how much you know but how much you do not know too.

Let me tell you a story, even though some of you know it already because I like to tell it. I got my doctorate from Columbia University. I worked hard for it and made tough sacrifices. I was walking down the hallway with my diploma in my hands, very proud of myself. I had finally made it. I was very arrogant. At that point, a door opened and students came out. They had just taken their qualifying examination for a doctorate degree. That is the exam that you take before writing your dissertation.

The day that I got my doctorate I was already obsolete.

I asked them if I could see the exam questions. I was shocked. I would have failed that exam if I had sat for it.

The day that I got my doctorate I was already obsolete.

To be leaders of the future do not be dogmatic: "I have a plan, I know which way I am going and that is it." No! You have to be extremely flexible. You have to be extremely humble. You must admit to yourself what you do not know. This means that you are willing to learn from others all the time. And from whom do you have to learn the most? From the people down below. The workers. The people on the line.

The rule of health is listen to your body. The day you stop listening to your body you become sick. Managers, listen to your organization! Leaders, listen to the organization! The higher you climb up the company's hierarchy, the smaller your mouth should be and the bigger your ears. Listen because you do not know. That will be your strength.

Good education should teach you how much you do not know rather than how much you know. That means that good management education is not about teaching you to know but teaching you to be. Be a person who is open-minded, humble, a good listener, willing to admit mistakes, willing to surround yourself with people who are better than you.

I am very disappointed with management education as practiced today. We have to change our education. I was a professor at UCLA, Columbia, and Stanford, as well as Tel Aviv University and Jerusalem University. I gave up my professorship and my tenure because I was disgusted with management education. The reason is that the natural sciences have penetrated the social sciences in a dysfunctional way. The prevalent logic is that you should quantify, measure everything. People get promoted on the basis of statistical analyses of answers to questionnaires. In order to quantify they need to narrow their inquiry to limited factors while the managerial reality is fuzzy; and, moreover, critical areas of management are not quantifiable.

The quantitative approach has penetrated education so deeply that it has put an end to thinking. People are not thinking anymore. Developing questionnaires and doing statistical analyses is very mechanistic thinking.

A quantitative analysis is fine but it can only be a tool, not a purpose. What we need is qualitative thinking, although qualitative thinking is fuzzy. There is nothing precise about it. This is why management and leadership are not only a science. There is very little science in it by the way. It is mostly art. You have to spend sleepless nights and make judgments and evaluations. You have to suffer because there is no clear answer to your problems. You just have to bite the bullet.

I observe that the discipline of general management has actually disappeared from management education. There is often only one course called Strategic Planning, but that is only one little piece of what is known as General Management.

Many years ago, I came to the conclusion that the perfect manager of an organization does not exist. We are trying to produce something that does not exist. It is a Fata Morgana. Why is that so? To manage any organization, be it a city, a country, a company, or a family, you need to produce results. You have to do that efficiently so that you do not waste resources. At the same time, you must think about the future and prepare the organization for it. This means that you have to be entrepreneurial. But you should also surround yourself with competent people and make them work as a team so that they do not waste energy fighting with each other. You want a constructive culture in your organization.

This means that we want a leader who is task-oriented, efficient, active, organized, systematic, motivated, ambitious, detail-oriented, creative, innovative, inspirational, sensitive...

In the prevalent management education that is called leadership development, we try to produce that person. There are not many of us around that fit this description, right? Because it does not exist. I have to tell you that the worst clients that I have had as a consultant are those who graduated from Harvard Business School. They are arrogant. They end up in private equity firms and consulting companies and start putting on airs.

What makes a good leader? Think of a family. It is very difficult to raise a child as a single parent, is it not? It takes a family, a man and a woman. It takes masculine and feminine energy. They have to complement each other.

Building a company is like building a family. You need a team whose members complement each other. You cannot do it on your own. That is why dictators destroy countries. That is why democracy is better. So who is a good leader? Somebody who is not afraid of working with people who are different. A leader must not be afraid of differences. A leader must not curse a rose because it has thorns. Try to learn something from the differences that you observe rather than being afraid of them. This takes mutual respect and trust. Team members should be like the fingers of a hand: different yet united. They should not be united despite of being different, but because of being different. When we are different, we learn from each other. Our differences make us stronger.

Can you command respect and trust? Are you a person who can work with different people? If you are, you can be a leader of the future. That leader is not one who has a degree and is knowledgeable. If you think you know everything and you can predict the future, you are in trouble.

There is another problem with education. What does it teach you? How to maximize profits. As a consequence, profit has become a religion in our education. That is what we teach in finance, strategic planning, marketing... It is all about how to measure and achieve profit. That is the ultimate goal.

Milton Friedman got a Nobel Prize for turning profit into a religion. But do you know what this is doing to us? It is destroying our environment. By trying to obtain more and more profit, we produce more and more things that we do not need. In California, where I live, people have enormous houses and three cars each in their garages, and they are still miserable because it is not enough. They want more. But more is not better. It is worse. By trying to have more we destroy the world that we live in.

I do not mean to say that profit should be ignored. I have been a consultant to several socially conscious organizations, like The Body Shop. They all got in serious trouble because they ignored profit. Do not ignore profit! But accept that there should be a limit to it. You need it so that you can survive and grow. The real goal must be different: make a better world. Make it a better place to be.

I just came from Montenegro where I was an advisor to the central bank.

The bank's executive director took me to the village where he was born, in the north of the country. He introduced me to his brother. I asked him how he felt in that small mountain village of 3,000 people. He said, "Great!" I wondered how one could feel great in such a small place. He answered, "I have a roof over my head. I have food. I have *rakia* to drink. What am I missing?"

I hear more laughter in a developing country in one day than in a whole year in a developed country. As the standard of living goes up, the quality of life goes down. Which of the two is more important?

The leaders of the future must have a different set of values. We need a new value system in which less is beautiful. Less is better. Small is wonderful.

WHAT SHOULD BE THE GOAL OF A CORPORATION?[1]

ECONOMISTS AND CONSERVATIVE POLITICIANS say the goal of a business is profits—long-term profits. It is an easy goal to have because it is a clear one. It is measurable. It represents the interests of the owners. But it has a problem nonetheless. What are profits in the long term? How long is long? "In the long run, we are all dead," said John Maynard Keynes, the revered economist.

> *Economists and conservative politicians say the goal of a business is profits.*

How do you operationalize the long run, especially when CEOs are measured by quarterly earnings per share? Even managers of private companies feel the pressure to perform in the short run, simply because their competitors do.

Another school of thought, often supported by those on the political Left, is that the goal is to optimize the needs of a host of constituents: owners, labor, clients, community, etc. Although this goal fits the mood of the time and is politically correct, it is difficult to quantify. How does one optimize the interests of various constituents? That's an endless subject for discussion and argument.

Then what should the goal be?

Developmental psychology and the science of biology tell us that the purpose of every living system is survival and reproduction—in other words, the survival of the species.

What does that mean for corporations? Corporations are living systems, thus, they have an equivalent goal: the survival of the system in the long

1. Adizes Insights, November 2012.

run. The field of sociology supports the idea that the goal of all organizations is survivability.

This raises several questions: First, if we want to use living systems as an analogy for corporations and other organizations, how should we define "survival of the species?" What is the species in our analogy? The company itself? The industry the company belongs to? Or is the species the corporate institution as such?

The second question is no less complicated: How can we operationalize this goal so that it can be used as a management tool rather than a mere academic exercise?

In answer to the first question, I suggest that the "species" is the company itself, because that is what the CEO must focus on when making decisions. What will best promote the survival of the company he or she leads? The species could also be the industry—if an industry-wide organization with a leader has been established. In those circumstances, that leader has the same responsibility as any company CEO: to support and advance that industry's survival.

Let us address the second question. How should a leader go about securing the survival of the species he is entrusted with?

Well, how does anyone survive? How does a human being survive? Or a dog, or a cat, or a horse, or a tree, for that matter? By being healthy. A system that is not healthy will not survive in the long run, nor will it reproduce itself as effectively as a system that is healthy.

I suggest that the goal of every system—and that includes corporations and not-for-profit organizations, micro, mezzo, and macro systems—is to be and to remain healthy.

Confronted with major strategic decisions, or even some tactical decisions that have strategic repercussions, a leader should ask herself: Is my decision going to promote or impair the health of the system I lead?

Simple, right? Now the question is: How?

Those readers who know my theory of PAEI should not be surprised at my answer. If a system is:

- effective in the short run, i.e., it fulfills the purpose of its existence at the present time, which means satisfying the present needs of its clients, (P);

- effective in the long run, i.e., it works proactively to identify the future needs of both its existing clients and its new clients, and is preparing at present to satisfy those future needs, (E);

- efficient in the short run, i.e., it prevents the waste of energy, which we all know is fixed, (A); and, finally,

- efficient in the long run, i.e., it is organic, which means it is integrated both within itself and within its environment, (I),

then we have a healthy system—a PAEI system.

The goal of every leader, of any type of organization, is to strive to ensure that the PAEI roles are fulfilled and balanced correctly, and reflect the organization's phase in its lifecycle.

If a company is healthy, it will be profitable in the long run and will reproduce itself by bringing successful new products into new markets.

Change and Its Repercussions for the Banking Industry[1]

Abstract

CHANGES HAVE ALWAYS EXISTED but their speed and frequency have become rather apparent. Changes are present in all areas of life, but here we focus on those happening in the banking industry. Banks are undergoing revolutionary changes and they must change or perish in their present form. The article explains why banks must change and what are the threats to both asset and liability sides they would face otherwise. Changes result in modifications of strategies, organizations and management. The article concludes that banks that are the most flexible and able to adapt will win the day.

Change has been ever-present for millions of years, ever since the Big Bang, and probably before that as well. So, what is new today that we can say about change?

What is new about change in modern life is its speed and frequency. It keeps accelerating without even a pause to let us adapt, adjust or embrace the rapid changes that continue to define us and our society.

Furthermore, change today is different from its earlier forms, not only in velocity but in its very nature. For one thing, it is multifaceted. And multidisciplinary. And very, very much interconnected. The environment itself is becoming increasingly interwoven: technological changes impact our laws which, in turn, affect our social, cultural and economic systems, and not necessarily in the same order or even in ways that coalesce smoothly and naturally.

Instead, change in one institution often topples others like falling dominos.

---

1. Originally published in the *Journal of Central Banking Theory and Practice*, Volume 3, Issue 1 (January 2014).

Take the internet, for example, a technological innovation which has had profound economic repercussions.

E-commerce facilitated by the internet has replaced traditional retailing. Bookstores are closing left and right. Amazon now not only sells books, it has broadened into music and films, and beyond popular culture, to the point where it now markets whatever can be retailed, including food. It has revolutionized the retail industry.

But the internet has also had social repercussions. Traditional educational institutions find themselves threatened by new schools of learning and new forms of instruction which are growing like mushrooms via the internet.

> *The new communication technology has, in effect, become the handmaiden of revolution.*

And it does not end there. The new forms of communication have also generated popular uprisings and have helped unseat political governments. Facebook and Twitter are credited with contributing to the Arab Spring by spreading information instantly, so that citizens were galvanized into immediate action. And each situational change within the political dynamic is spread directly and at the push of a button to the ever-growing concerned populace. The new communication technology has, in effect, become the handmaiden of revolution.

What about the banking industry?

The business side of traditional banking has been built around the idea of taking savings and giving loans... and making a profit on the difference between what it pays for savings and what it charges for loans.

In 1982, when I was consulting for Bank of America we came to the conclusion that this scope of activity was under major threat; that banking was undergoing some important changes and if it remained static, committed exclusively to this product line, it would experience serious challenges to its survival. The prediction was proven right; one example being the bankruptcies running into billions of dollars of the savings and loans institutions a few years later.

Why did banking have to change?

On the liability side, instead of putting its money into a savings account, the public was offered many other financial opportunities to increase its economic holdings. On the asset side, suddenly there was competition from non-banking institutions such as private equity funds and the stock market, which could provide capital in place.

Threatened by both the asset and liability side, banks had to change. They converted from providing only traditional banking services into a more complex financial services corporation. Revenue was now derived from service fees, rather than only from the difference in the margins between loans and savings.

It also became clear that computerization and mobile banking could lend an unexpected flexibility to banking. A bank could now be mobile, located any place where a computer could be installed and an ATM made available for transactions.

These changes have had a revolutionary impact on the banking industry over the past thirty years.

For instance, Banco Azteka from Mexico, where I serve as a consultant, has trained and dispatched mobile bankers. They are men and women who come to your home, computer in hand, and offer banking services: extend personal and mortgage loans, open savings or checking accounts, and, in effect, bring the bank into your home.

It has become possible to set up a table with a computer and a banner and establish a bank branch wherever there is traffic and people congregate. So retail chains today rent space to banks so that they can set up tables and/or counters and open for business, especially for customer credit, in places as different from the old banking structures as large food stores and pharmacies.

Banks used to look like big citadels. They were viewed as a place to safeguard money. No more. An open environment—inviting, friendly, accessible, able to provide services—had to replace the austere, guardian structures of the past.

The change in strategy, in what now constitutes the financial services business instead of legacy banking business, has had an impact on the organizational structure of banks: product managers are now needed to manage different product lines and different marketing departments are suddenly necessary to manage the diverse market segments. This has created a matrix organization with all the inevitable accompanying complexities.

There are new managerial problems that need to be addressed. For example, where in the organizational structure should we center the bank's profit responsibility? It is complicated because there is uncertainty about the loan inventory. How solid and reliable is it? How large are the bad debts? How much of the profits should be viewed as a reserve against future losses?

Banco Azteka has made risk management responsible for the bank's profitability. It is an innovation, and perhaps a daring one. But come to think of it, the idea makes sense. If the risk taken is too high, it will impact profitability in the long run.

The next question is the role of the branches. Where do they belong in the organizational chart? Many branches serve both the small middle market and the larger retail market; and even at times, the corporate market. In that case, where are the branches in the chart? They should not report either to small business or to retailing because they serve both.

They have to be separate from the market segment and from the product line. They become something like a retail outlet for a myriad of products. But that calls for a retraining of the branch manager. He or she is not the loan officer anymore. He or she manages a "supermarket" of services and the role has been transformed into client relations for whatever product is needed.

The banking industry is going through a revolution of sorts. Technological innovations as well as major changes in the financial industry have given banks little choice. They must change or perish in their present form.

Banks that are most flexible and able to adapt will win the day. This flexibility cannot, of course, be at the cost of violating compliance. The organizational structure of the bank needs, on one hand, strong quality control of operations, and at the same time flexibility to adapt to a fast changing environment. Not an easy assignment.

PART IV

✣

MANAGEMENT STYLES

Attitude for Mutual Trust and Respect[1]

MUTUAL TRUST AND RESPECT have always played a central role in my thinking and, of course, in many of my books. The reason is simple: They provide the compelling underpinnings that all systems need in order to be successful. By all systems I mean everything from an individual (in which case it becomes self respect and self trust), a family, a business, a society, or even a macro system such as a nation state. I would suggest that the concept applies to the world as a system as well.

It behooves us, then, to know how to create and nourish MT&R. If we fail to focus on trust and respect, neglect to work on them continuously, our system—be it an individual, business organization, or society—will be eroded by change.

That becomes serious. Why? It is important that we place change at the forefront of our thinking. Change is not just any force, but can be destructive enough to cause disintegration. Simply stated, it is a force that generates entropy. So, to keep any (and every) system healthy, integration—what I call negative entropy—is required. And that is what MT&R does: It integrates.

In my books I have elaborated on ways to build MT&R, and at the Adizes Institute we have created a program built on four factors that help develop MT&R:

1) common vision and values;

2) functional structure;

3) collaborative decision-making process; and

4) mature people.

1. Adizes Insights August 2013.

In this insight we will focus on the last variable: people. What kind of people grant and command respect and trust.

In my book *How to Solve the Mismanagement Crisis*[2] I point out the essential role that mature managers play in solving a variety of crises. When you finish analyzing organizational structures and departmental strategies you are still left with the problem of which men and women are best able to carry out the necessary changes. Invariably, after citing requisite skills and experience, I realized the necessary factor was a human being who was considered mature.

There are nine factors that my research shows mature people possess:

1) performs all PAEI roles, at least to the threshold level;
2) knows his/her strengths and weaknesses;
3) accepts feedback from others;
4) possesses a balanced view of him/herself;
5) understands who he/she is;
6) identifies excellence in others in areas where he/she is weak;
7) recognizes the judgment of others in areas where his/her knowledge is limited (controlled ego);
8) resolves conflicts constructively;
9) creates a learning environment.

Here are some interesting quotes that caught my attention. They seem to me to reflect the right attitude of what I call mature people. I do not know the author of the first quote. If anyone recognizes the source, please let me know.

> Live without pretending,
> Love without depending,
> Listen without defending,
> Speak without offending.

Here is another one:

> Give up speed.
> Give up greed.
> Be suspicious of urgency,
> and
> Be curious, not critical.
>
> –JIM MOTT

2. Santa Barbara: Adizes Institute Publications 1985.

> You can be rich by having more than you need,
> Or by needing less than you have.
> – JIM MOTT

And my favorite:

> God, grant me the serenity to accept the things I cannot change,
> Courage to change the things I can,
> And wisdom to know the difference.
> – REINHOLD NIEBUHR

How about this one:

> Those whom the Gods would destroy, they first make drunk with
> power.
> – CHARLES A. BEARD

I hope you find these thoughts helpful as you explore ways to develop MT&R.

COLLABORATION VS. COOPERATION[1]

ARE COLLABORATION AND COOPERATION the same thing? Are they synonymous? I believe they are different, and that the differences can be seen by looking at the Adizes map of managing change.[2]

Collaboration is what a complementary team does. It works together, learning from one another, cross-pollinating. For collaboration to occur, mutual respect is necessary. Once respect exists, the condition for learning from one another is established. At that point, if the parties have something to contribute to one another, collaboration might happen.

Notice that I say it *might* happen. For collaboration to be achieved, respect and resourcefulness are necessary conditions, but they are not sufficient. A positive, supportive climate is also necessary for learning and cross-pollination to occur. For that, a prescribed, structured, systemic process of deliberation is required. It should ensure that there is a positive climate for the dynamics of the collaboration.

Cooperation is a totally different thing. Cooperation is located on the right side of the Adizes map. Its focus is not on decision making, for which collaboration is necessary, but on implementation of the decision made. To implement a decision that involves change, a commonality of interests among all the parties necessary for implementation is a must.

As we can see, for collaboration, respect is called for. For cooperation, trust is called for.

Cooperation will occur when there is a common interest, or when a common interest is perceived to exist in the long run, which requires both faith and trust.

1. Adizes Insights, May 2011.

2. Ichak Adizes. *Mastering Change.* Santa Barbara: Adizes Institute Publications, 1991.

As we can see, for collaboration, respect is called for. For cooperation, trust is called for.

Trust *and* respect, collaboration *and* cooperation, are necessary for managing change without destructive conflict, for making effective decisions, and for implementing them efficiently.

ON MALICIOUS OBEDIENCE[1]

I HAVE JUST LEARNED ABOUT A CONCEPT I did not have a name for until now: malicious obedience.

Malicious obedience is when you, as a subordinate, know a decision given to you is a disaster and you execute it to its complete finalization anyway.

Why would you execute a decision that you know will be a disaster?

To discredit your boss.

Malicious obedience can backfire. Many managers know how to pass blame on to others very well. If you are ever going to implement a decision you know will be a disaster, be sure to get the instruction in writing. You should inform the person giving you the order that you are against the decision but you will execute it once you get that order in writing.

You have protected yourself, but the question should be asked: Why would you do it anyway? Why the obedience to a decision you oppose?

Because you are malicious. You believe that it will hurt the decision maker more than whoever is impacted by the decision will be harmed.

Malicious obedience, to me, is the utmost in disintegration.

I admit I have not experienced malicious obedience, but I suspect it happens in highly hierarchical, autocratic organizations, where the rejection of superiors is high and the animosity cannot be released.

A person who is scared not to implement a decision will execute it to the most detailed component (obedience) and watch the organization suffer (that is where the maliciousness comes in). It is like payback: The

1. Adizes Insights, April 2012.

employee gives back to the organization that has made him suffer. It is like revenge.

Malicious obedience, to me, is the utmost in disintegration. Usually a clear sign of disintegration is that decisions that were made are not executed, or are not executed in the spirit they were made. Here we have the opposite: The decision was executed down to the tiniest detail, with disastrous repercussions.

The conclusion I am arriving at here is that disintegration can have multiple faces and one has to watch not only what happens but also why it happens.

The Relationship of Uncertainty, Risk, and Mutual Trust and Respect[1]

I HAVE BEEN WONDERING FOR YEARS how these concepts are related to each other. Here is my insight. If you will pardon the play on words, change is constant, which means that something new always makes an appearance; it comes into being. That new entity—I will use a consulting term and call it a new phenomenon—needs to be addressed.

We usually call the new phenomenon "a problem" because we need to deal with it, one way or another. What does it mean to "deal with it?"

First, we must decide what to do. The emphasis is on *decide*, and doing nothing counts as a decision.

Second, we must implement our decision. It sounds simple, but do not be fooled. Sometimes we decide but fail to implement. Think of dieting and exercising. And sometimes we act (i.e., implement) without deciding. Like becoming angry. We are just angry. We did not decide to be angry.

The point I am making is that these two actions, deciding and implementing, are two separate behaviors.

What is involved in making a decision? Let us assume, for example, there is a problem caused by change. A new baby enters the family; or a new parent. Or, to change the venue, a new CEO or plant manager. Or there is a change in the market due to increased competition or new technology. All of these constitute what we might refer to as change.

So now it is decision time. When it comes to making a decision about something new, there is almost always uncertainty because there are few guides and less information than we would like. We want to know everything possible before we act, before we endeavor to solve a new problem

1. Adizes Insights, May 2013.

caused by change. Alas, complete information is never available. Thus, uncertainty.

What is involved in implementing a decision? Risk. Even if we try to play it safe, some amount of risk is present. In effect, a decision is not risky until implemented. And, I repeat, not acting is a form of action, and thus risky too.

Why is there risk? Because we are trying to solve a problem that is new, and there is no proven track record guaranteeing success.

The presence and pressure of uncertainty and risk often lead to the conclusion that change is stressful. So it is not strange that we try to resist change as much as possible.

Is there a way to reduce uncertainty and risk, and thus make change more palatable?

Is there a way to reduce uncertainty and risk, and thus make change more palatable? There is. Adopt a problem-solving strategy where decisions are made by a complementary team—complementary not only in know-how but also in their styles. It is a significant way to reduce uncertainty. The team members will teach each other. They will share a variety of experiences, knowledge, and judgments.

For effective implementation they will explore and look for common interests among those whose cooperation is necessary for implementation. If there is common interest risk will be lower than if there is no common interest. Without common interest there is the possibility that some of those needed for implementation will not cooperate, or might even sabotage the solution, thus increasing the risks involved.

But, it is not that simple. This is not the end of the diagnosis.

Complementary teams who should learn from each other, and should have a common interest, will certainly have conflicts. After all, learning from others who disagree with you is stressful, and an ongoing common interest is a utopian expectation.

Unless there is mutual trust and respect. That is the key. If there is trust, a culture of give and take, interests will balance over time. There will be faith that common interests do exist. Respect for each other's differences, and a willingness to listen to and honor the opinions of others are also necessary. As we learn from one another, the process reduces uncertainty. Only through such respect can we learn from diversity.

The end result is that mutual trust and respect reduce uncertainty and risk, and, in the process, enable faster action and paths to change.

Those companies that have a culture of MT&R will adapt to change faster and better than those that do not. They will succeed and flourish in times of change, while those without MT&R will stagnate and eventually disappear.

The purpose of the Adizes Institute is to provide the tools for organizations to transform their culture into one that develops and nourishes mutual trust and respect, and, in so doing, make the company the champion of its industry and nation as measured by profitability and by loyalty of the employees to the company.

What Is a Real Asset?[1]

IN A SEMINAR THAT WE JOINTLY TAUGHT in Moscow, David Tice, a friend and professor of business at the University of California, Berkeley, made a point on strategic planning which was illuminating. I want to share it with you.

What is a real asset of a company? For instance, he asked, what is the real asset of an oil company? Most people will say their oil reserves. Professor Tice said that the real asset is the one you cannot sell.

This is very important: "The asset you cannot sell."

Reserves can be sold. Machinery can be sold. People can be fired and new workers hired.

The real asset is the one you cannot sell.

So what is it that cannot be sold? It is your connections. Your corporate DNA. Your culture. Your reputation. Your values.

It complemented my lecture on what makes a good leader: not what he or she has, but what he or she is. And what a person is—his or her character, integrity, values, style, and behavior—cannot be sold.

All of this relates significantly to building a culture of mutual trust and respect. This is an enormous, time-consuming task. At times it is even painful because you need, as a leader, to swim against the current. The "current," the normal way people behave, leads to disintegration, not integration.

To love, respect, and try to solve problems constructively, with maturity, is much more difficult than to hate and complain and spread rumors.

---

1. Adizes Insights, July 2013.

How many people watch a high-rise being built? Now imagine how many watch it being demolished. Making war is so much easier than making peace. Staying in a marriage is much more difficult that getting divorced.

Unfortunately, these very real assets—culture and values—are difficult to measure and evaluate. Usually they appear under the heading "goodwill" in accounting. They appear as a high multiple of earnings per share. But for many economists, culture and values are too "soft" to be weighed or considered as reliable measures. Economists (like bankers) want hard assets that can be sold. The rest is "air" for them.

Many CEOs hire a consultant to improve the way the production line operates, or to find new clients, or to cut costs. Only the very enlightened understand that the real asset is the culture of the company and investing in it is the most important corporate move to undertake.

What makes a good marriage? How many cars we have? How many homes we have? Or is it the nature of our relationship, as a family?

The most valuable asset is the one we do not see but feel. The one you cannot sell but, luckily, you can develop.

PART V

❋

ORGANIZATIONS
AND
LIFECYCLES

BUREAUCRATIC COMMUNICATION[1]

I HAVE ALREADY DESCRIBED, in my book *Managing Corporate Lifecycles*,[2] how an aging organization behaves. In this essay I would like to focus on one aspect of aging systems: how they communicate.

The first time I noticed how people in a bureaucracy communicate was during Communist party meetings in Yugoslavia in the 1960s. At the time, I thought it was funny to listen to people talk during those meetings. The sentences were long and convoluted. The choice of words was bombastic. Then, I attended meetings of aging companies in my consulting work in the United States, and the pattern looked familiar.

Now, years later, I am consulting in Russia. They formally denounced Communism over twenty years ago, but I noticed the same pattern of communication in meetings.

The pattern I describe below apparently is not driven by political affiliation or credo, nor by culture, but by location on the lifecycle.

First, what is the pattern? I describe some of it in my book. In a young, growing company the pattern of communication is direct and short. Using four-letter words is not unheard of. In my experience, cursing and calling people by derogatory names is frequent in a Go-Go company. At the same time, there is a lot of laughter. It is an (E) culture. (E)s are very, very aggressive—even offensive—then the next day they are charming, relaxed, and funny. They forget the rage with which they communicated the day before. The culture of the company reflects the style of its leader.

In an aging company, especially a bureaucratic one, the opposite is

1. Adizes Insights, August 2012.

2. Santa Barbara: Adizes Institute Publications, 2004.

happening. No one offends anyone. The communication pattern is formal. And confusing.

To impress their audience they use "heavy" words, in the sense that sometimes you have to open a dictionary to find out what the word means. They will repeat themselves, but the repetition does not make their communication clearer. Just the opposite: It makes it more confusing. They will speak in circles, where the next sentence negates the message of the previous sentence or paragraph. They do not speak directly, the way a Go-Go will, but as if insinuating something.

People communicate, but what they say can have multiple interpretations.

Bombastic statements are not rare. They are the norm. Statements that communicate glory, big size, and extreme devotion are repeated. The statements reflect the total culture of grandiosity. Have you seen the buildings erected during Stalin era in Moscow? I cannot describe the architecture—one has to see it. It is enormous. It dwarfs you, overpowers you. It is not just Soviet architecture that reveals a certain culture, the communication pattern does the same. It is mostly form while function takes a backseat.

Another point: A bureaucratic organization is disintegrated. The left hand does not know what the right hand is doing. That is reflected in their communication pattern too. One just does not understand what the speaker is saying. It all sounds like he or she took sentences and put them in a random sequence. I once transcribed such a meeting and moved sentences around. You would not know which paragraph actually was used. None of them made much sense anyway.

People in meetings often intimidate each other. In a Go-Go company a person might start his message by saying: "I am sick and tired of this discussion. We discussed it many times before. Nothing gets done here anyway. We are wasting time…" Or "This is too insignificant. Why are we spending so much time on it," etc. These sentences are a way of intimidating the listeners, to change the topic, or get them to yield to the speaker's opinion.

You will not ever hear such sentences in an aging company. In an aging company, the intimidation happens very subtly. They stab each other with a knife, but it is laced with honey.

Here is how I noticed it is done in Russia. During the Communist regime everyone was a "Comrade." Russians do not address anyone as "Comrade" anymore. It was substituted with the word "colleague," but it is said in the same tone of voice as "Comrade." The way to intimidate is to say, "May I react to my learned colleague?" or "Colleagues, let us move on."

A culture driven by location on the lifecycle is reflected not only in the strategy of the company, not only in its financial statements and processes, but also in the architecture of their office, in the use of space, in the selection of furniture, in the dress code, and in communication patterns.

Culture is reflected in everything the company does.

Control vs. Diversity[1]

IN WORKING WITH A RUSSIAN CLIENT, I had an experience similar to the one I had working with the Ministry of Health of Ghana over forty years ago. In Russia I was structuring the regional organization for a client that had seventeen territories all over the country.

When I would structure region Y, the client would be in disagreement with the structure because it did not fit that of region X. So we proceeded to structure region X. Now he was in deep doubt whether it was the right structure for X because it did not fit Y. This gave me an illumination: The client was trying to find a template with which all the regions could be structured the same way. Ah, this Soviet Union legacy of sameness.

Why are they so attached to sameness? What is the source of this cultural bias?

I realized then that I had the same experience in Ghana forty years ago. The British Imperialists structured the public service in all their colonies the same way: for control. During the colonial era, when a foreign service official was trained in Britain he was trained so he could serve anywhere in the world, in any territory, without much difficulty because all ministries, all public service organizations, were structured the same way all over the world.

In the Soviet Union, apparently, the same practice ruled: sameness to get maximum control from the center, from the Kremlin.

In structuring the territories for this Russian client, I was trying to convince him that each territory should be structured as it makes sense to that territory. The distances are different, the communication complexities

1. Adizes Insights, August 2012.

are different. Many cities in Russia have no direct air transport connection. You have to fly to Moscow to connect to the other city. (Moscow is the hub for all of Russia in more ways than one.)

The VP in charge of the territories was very uncomfortable with structural diversity, so I asked myself: Why in the West, in a market economy, are we comfortable with such diversity?

My insight is that in a capitalist society we seek performance more than control. We measure the performance of a territory, and if we need to accept its indigenous reasons to be different in order to increase performance, so be it. We do not care what you do (within limits of the law and ethics) as long as you perform.

Why are they so attached to sameness?

In totalitarian systems it is not performance that calls the shots, it is control. Control first and above all. In this case, performance suffers. It is not strange then that the Russian economy, and, for that matter, all Communist countries' economies, suffered from poor economic performance.

That was true for colonial Britain, too. Performance of the colonies was less important than being controlled from London. When the colonies were emancipated they remained structured for control, which undermined their capability to maximize performance. Or, as I have said in many of my lectures, what is bad about colonialism is not what they took out, but what they left behind: a culture of maximizing control at the expense of performance.

The above insight has more to it. What I am describing above is the conflict between effectiveness and efficiency, i.e., between diversity and controllability. Efficiency can increase profitability as long as it does not decrease effectiveness to the point of sub-optimization.

Increase efficiency, but watch what is happening to effectiveness. At a certain point (using marginal analysis) you might find out that one more unit of efficiency will decrease overall profitability because of the loss in effectiveness.

The Greek Debt Crisis[1]

G REECE'S MAIN PROBLEM IS NOT DEBT. Other countries have an equal percentage of debt to GNP—some even higher. But they are not in a crisis. So, what is the problem in Greece? It is its inability to *pay* its debt, to honor its financial commitments. In other words, the debt crisis is the *manifestation* of the problem. If we want to decide what needs to be done, we must look for the cause.

I believe there were several causes.

First, Greece has a huge, expensive government apparatus, employing many people with lots of high-priced benefits. It is all (A) and no (P). Meanwhile, the productive sector, such as the shipping industry, is either exempt from paying taxes or is successfully evading them. The result is that the government spends more than it collects.

What covered the difference up to now? Debt financing combined with subsidies from the European Union. Obviously, there must be an end both to the amount of debt a country can take on, and to how long that country can reasonably rely on subsidies. That end—better known as the debt crisis—has arrived.

This practice of relying on debt to finance non-productive parts of a government system has also had social repercussions. It has created a culture of dependency. People expect not to work very hard but to live well. In other words, they feel entitled to be non-productive and let someone else pay the bills.

How did this happen in the nation that gave birth to democracy?

Let it be said that the citizens of all democracies are grateful to Greece.

1. Adizes Insights, March 2012.

But it must also be said that, in the modern era, Greek politicians have abused democracy.

How? By awarding benefits to special interest groups to secure their votes. Those "entitled" special interests are how the government apparatus became obese, and also how many who could and should have paid taxes were given license not to pay.

As the root of the problem, I attribute the debt crisis to a flaw in the democratic system that enables mediocre and corrupt politicians to come to power, stay in power, and ultimately destroy the country.

It has created a culture of dependency.

Greece is not the only country suffering from the abuses of democracy. We in the United States, too, need to overhaul our system. It served us well for a while, but in the complex world we live in today, it can have more liabilities than assets.

The invisible hand of the market is too slow to react to changes that occur in a complex environment at a rapid rate. Economic theory that assumes the system will seek its equilibrium has to assume a low rate of change. At the current rate of change, the system cannot cope. "Things fall apart; the centre cannot hold," Yeats wrote more than ninety years ago, but he might have been talking about democracy in the twenty-first century.

We need a new theory of democracy—what I would call regulated democracy—a system that takes into account the complexity, the interdependency, and the high rate of change in modern times.

In the meantime, what should Greece do? For one: Go on a starvation diet, which means significantly slashing the ranks of government employees. Two: Change the tax code and improve tax collection. Three: Severely punish corruption. And four: Make loans easily available to small businesses and start-ups.

In other words, cut (A), increase (P), and stimulate (E), while giving hope to the people by electing technocrats to positions of leadership of the country. Bring in new faces, a new generation of leaders who are honest and capable. What Greece needs more than ever is hope based on trust and respect—to build (I)!

GREECE[1]

THIS WEEKEND, JUNE 2, 2013, I was invited to meet with a group of businessmen, politicians, and media people to diagnose the problems of the country and to express my opinion of what needs to be done.

Below is the illumination, which I believe can bring some additional light for those interested. (In order to diagnose and design a potential plan of action I am using my lifecycle theory[2] and the PAEI theory.[3])

Location on lifecycle

Greece is in premature aging, close to the recrimination stage where different parties have a destructive fight. Greece avoided falling into the recrimination stage, for now, by establishing a coalition of three major parties to run the country—a good move that should arrest a dangerous deterioration of the situation.

That Greece is apparently in premature aging is indicated by the following potential improvement points:

- The culture does not honor rules. There is no rule of law, therefore, laws are made and not applied.

- The judicial system is not effective. Some major business interests (oligarchs) are above the law (no lawyer dares to sue them), and antitrust laws are not applied. Many laws are badly written, overlapping, and inconsistent.

---

1. Adizes Insights, June 2013.

2. For the theory of lifecycles see Ichak Adizes: *Managing Corporate Lifecycles.* (Santa Barbara: Adizes Institute Publications, 2004).

3. For the PAEI theory see Ichak Adizes: *The Ideal Executive: Why You Cannot Be One and What to Do About It.* (Santa Barbara: Adizes Institute Publications, 2004).

- Greece has political dynasties: The nephew or son of the previous prime minister becomes the next prime minister, or the daughter of another prime minister becomes the new minister of foreign affairs (similar to a family trap in business organizations).

In addition to the lack of rule of law—weak (A)—Greece lacks a culture of constructive dialogue and has little experience with teamwork—low (I). This causes a bloated, inefficient bureaucracy, overlapping ministries, and too many public servants for functions that, in other countries, one tenth as many people perform.

The lack of rule of law also causes economic interests (oligarchs) to have an undue influence on the government via financial support in election time and by controlling the media. The government, in return, controls the banks that loan to the oligarchs. The end result is that banks loan more to the big business interests than to the middle class, which is slowly disappearing.

Another way the oligarchs benefit from no rule of law is by monopolizing contracts for government development projects.

As expected from its location on the lifecycle, the Greek government has no vision or clear long-term plans. They are caught in a cycle of tactical decision making, trying to survive and meet the demands of the Troika (the European Central Bank, International Monetary Fund, and the European Commission), which, in order to give them loans, requires that the Greek government cut public spending. The government did so, not by increasing efficiency of the bureaucracy but by cutting salaries and pensions across the board. This has caused consumption to plummet, triggering negative economic growth.

The end result is that there is even less of revenue to collect. To start with, taxes were not well collected, partly because the rich had ways to avoid paying, and now, on top of that, there are fewer people who earn enough to pay anything. That causes the gap between what the government spends and what the government collects not to be closed in a sustainable way.

The result of all this is that health and education services have seriously deteriorated, there is a high unemployment rate, a brain drain, hate between the public service sector and the private sector, and a population that is becoming rebellious. (While I was in Athens, three bombs exploded in offices of various commissions.)

Observations

Greek culture has a soul. Listen to their music. Watch them dance their circular dances. Watch them interact. It is like one large family.

But Greece has also a very individualistic and (E)ntrepreneuring culture, a result of which is little mutual trust and respect. Everyone is trying to prove that he or she is smarter than the other one, and they are fiercely competitive. (Watch their TV debates. You do not have to understand the language, just watch the interaction.)

Without mutual trust and respect, Greece can deteriorate to serious dis-integration manifested by internal terrorism and street riots. They have proven in the past they are prone to that. After the Second World War they even had a civil war.

The economic crisis is a change which, as should be anticipated, releases centrifugal forces to action: The very extreme right-wing party and the coalition of leftist parties both are growing at the expense of the centrist parties. It can lead to a confrontation. A breakdown. Or they can join forces and undermine democracy.

So far the manifestations of the disintegration are mild: street riots, man-ifestations that block traffic. The suicide rate is on the rise but crime is not. The divorce rate is not on the rise either. Apparently because the society still has hope that somehow they will pull out. That hope is fed by the government and the oligarchs through the media. The government controls the media through the banks. (The media is in deep debt to the banks, which are controlled by the government.) The business interests I referred to before (oligarchs), also influence the media because they con-tribute a significant amount of the revenues of the media through buying advertising for their endeavors. Their interest is also not to experience turbulence. So the business interests and the political interests silence the media and no bad news is reported.

Add to this the fact that summer is coming—and with it a large inflow of tourism—and the future as of now does not look so bleak. But, come winter, if there is no improvement in the economic environment, or some indication of economic growth and improvement in employment rates, it is hard to predict that peace will continue.

There is also a problem with the present solutions imposed by the Troika. The people who work there are mainly trained as macro economists.

For them the way to solve the problem is to cut labor costs, to cut salaries and the bureaucracy, which will make Greece competitive. That will bring investments in and the problem will be solved. When you only have a hammer as a tool, all problems look like a nail.

For investments to be made the cost of capital has to be low. Today in Greece it is about 15%. That is high and thus not very attractive.

The first thing to do is to remove from power those who are benefiting from the lack of rule of law. Having done so, the government should enforce antitrust laws and bring smaller companies, not those of the oligarchs, to bid on government projects so that a middle class will get stronger and economic wealth will be better spread out.

Greek culture has a soul.

Greece also needs to revamp its tax-collection procedures to increase harvesting of taxes fairly. At the same time, the government needs to design the vision of the country as far as which segments it wants to develop so that its portfolio of GNP looks less dependent on tourism.

Only then should the government cut the ranks of public servants and free the labor force to the new endeavors the government started according to the designed vision, thus turning fat into muscle.

This move requires investments.

Greece badly needs external investments but to be attractive to investors it needs rule of law, a judicial system that works, decentralization of economic power, de-bureaucratization of government, and government policies that encourage the right investments.

Beyond investments, Greece will need to retrain bureaucrats to become productive in industry. This is not easy or inexpensive. Where is the money coming from? So far, instead of investments we noticed vulture funds circling Greece trying to acquire assets at bottom prices.

Greece is not capable of running its own monetary policy. It is on the euro and thus cannot print money to encourage economic activity. This is a limitation and Greece must get the EU to invest in Greece and not just recapitalize the banks. Greece itself cannot generate the funds necessary for its economic growth. A type of Marshall Plan for Greece is called for. If this does not happen Greece will have to consider exiting the Eurozone and conducting its own monetary policy.

Whatever the Greek government does must be done in a way that reinforces the rule of law, and creates a civilized dialogue and cooperation, which are the cause of the problems Greece has. Just cutting salaries makes the numbers look good but does not attack the root cause of the problems.

Projection for the future

If Greece continues to make tactical, knee-jerk decisions, to meet the demands of the European Central Bank mechanistically—meeting the numbers but not dealing with the root cause of its troubles: the rule of law, de-bureaucratization, and decentralization of economic power— and does not get massive investments, there is a chance of major social disruption, crime, and disorder, which will dry up tourism and bring Greece further into trouble.

The road to recovery is not easy. The slippery road of becoming a third-world country is more probable.

In Search of the Absolute[1]

THIS WEEK I HAVE CONSULTED for the kibbutz movement in Israel.

The kibbutzim believe in equality, fairness, equal opportunity for all, sharing, and mutual support, among other great ideas. To fulfill this ideology every member in a kibbutz works with no salary. They get some allowance determined by the size of their family. That is all. Each member works in whatever way he or she is qualified or asked to work. Some work outside the kibbutz, like doctors in a hospital or managers of factories, and all of their income goes to the kibbutz. They get their equal allowance like anyone else. Healthcare is free. So are food and education.

We are only equal when we are dead.

This is how the movement started. Some still live this way, but they are a minority. Today the kibbutz is experiencing a lot of pressure to change. Members want freedom to choose. The allowance was increased and now members chose what to eat, for which they pay. Their allowance is also for buying clothes, which they chose. Some kibbutzim discontinued the equal allowance and now give different amounts, like a salary, to every member depending on the task they perform.

In other words, "equality" is not followed religiously anymore.

What happened? My insight is that whenever you have multiple incompatible factors in a dynamic situation, the absolute cannot exist. We are only equal when we are dead.

People ask for equality, for democracy, for love, for health, for happiness, and now I realize these concepts are vulnerable. With time they might deteriorate. They cannot be absolute.

1. Adizes Insights, April 2012.

Whenever multiple subsystems are involved, whenever multiple incompatible factors are involved, there cannot be a steady optimum, a steady equality. A workable equality, for instance, is where sometimes you are above and sometimes I am above, or you have more and I have less and another time the situation is reversed. It is like a trembling equilibrium. Take a marriage for instance. There can be no absolute equality on everything all the time. In reality, one time you win an argument and another time I win. That is a working equality.

It is a non-working equality when one is above the other permanently or continuously.

To be totally equal continuously means that there is no change. Only in death are we totally and continuously equal.

Those absolute concepts are a vision: We want them but they are never achievable, or, if achievable, they are not steady. They need to be maintained to be sustainable.

One has to continuously work to reach them and maintain that equilibrium that, with time, falls out of balance.

MAKING A MATRIX ORGANIZATION WORK[1]

MATRIX ORGANIZATIONS are usually prescribed and implemented in organizations where double responsibilities are expected on the same subject.

For example, although product managers are responsible for product profitability, they must rely on functions within the organization that they cannot control, such as salespeople and production workers who do not report to them.

Who, then, is responsible for the profits? The matrix organization is common in global companies. Such organizations need to think globally, but act locally. Who, then, is responsible for the profits: the local market, where the action is; or the global product manager, who probably directs pricing, product definition, and strategy?

One way to avoid this complexity is to make the global organization responsible for profits, while the local branch becomes just a sales organization—not responsible for profitability.

Or the opposite: Give the local market responsibility for profitability, while the global organization provides the functions of pricing, product definition, strategy, etc.

But both solutions, while they have the virtue of simplicity, fail to satisfy management's need to monitor people in the company and hold as many as possible responsible for profitability. This probably explains why organizations frequently switch back and forth from centralized operations to decentralized operations. But eventually, when they conclude

1. Adizes Insights, August 2011.

that neither structure provides the desired controllability and accountability, they either reorganize into a matrix organization, where the global and the local share responsibility; or they give up and organize themselves functionally, making the president alone responsible for profits.

In the latter case, both local and global organizations become cost centers with different goals to achieve. Local is responsible for sales but is not measured for profitability. And the global organization is measured by the function it is supposed to perform, but also is not accountable for profit.

Both solutions are problematic.

Matrix organizations create a lot of conflicts—particularly internal conflicts—because it is not clear who is in charge.

Another reason that organizing the global organization functionally is a bad idea is that profits are not measured by market or by product. As a result, profit accountability is measured through cost accounting, which does not identify which people should take responsibility for profitability. It gives information, but the question of who is in charge, who can make changes in order to improve results, is not answered.

What is the solution, then? To make a matrix organization that works. Here is how: You have to decide which unit is colored green and which is colored olive. What does this mean?

Let us take the example of global product management, with local sales and service management. Assume that both are profit centers.

In Adizes Methodology we color the org chart. Profit units are either green or olive colors. Green, however, is the one accountable for reaching profitability. It is the driving force. Olive, on the other hand, monitors profitability and alerts green if there is a problem.

Think of a green global manager and olive local market manager. The global product manager is responsible for profitability in all local markets. The local markets execute his or her plans. They are measured for profitability but the control of the variables that impact profitability, like price, quality, and product line diversity, are all decided by the global product manager.

Now reverse it: The markets are green and the global product manager is olive.

Who now decides price and impacts revenue and profitability? The market. The global product manager only monitors product profitability and alerts when there is a problem.

PAEI Code and Strategy Development[1]

Paei, AS I HAVE CLAIMED many times, is a code. It is the DNA of organizations. It can be used to analyze managerial styles, organizational structures, decision-making processes, and reward systems. It can be used to predict the sequence of problems organizations will have along their lifecycles.

PAEI can be also used to design corporate strategy by balancing the four roles for success: Which roles are the organization's strengths and which are its weaknesses, and thus what should management focus on for the future?

Let us look at this in more detail.

A company can have a strategy that capitalizes on:

- better service than the competition (P)
- cheaper cost of production and delivery (A)
- higher level of innovation (E)
- better organizational culture that attracts and retains better human capital (I)

Notice that this follows the code of PAEI and also that no one company can be the best in all four. It costs money to perform each role and thus can be prohibitively expensive in the aggregate. Like the myth of the ideal executive, there is no ideal or perfect company, performing all the roles at the highest possible level.

Southwest Airlines focuses on better service than the competition (P). Dell is characterized by cheaper costs (A). A higher rate of innovation (E) is what 3M relied on to beat the competition, and a great organizational culture (I) made HP stand out in its early days.

1. Adizes Insights, November 2011.

What will your strategy be? What do you naturally excel at? What has developed organically thus far that distinguishes you from the competition? Is it still relevant? Where is your industry on the lifecycle? If it is on the aging side of the curve you must watch your costs very carefully. But that is not enough. Start investing in innovation. And if innovation has run its course and is not an advantage anymore you have to transform your company from an (E) strategy to something else—(P), (A), or (I) strategy.

Take the semiconductor industry as an example in this regard: Innovation has hit the wall because we are at the end of our knowledge of physics. We cannot make our chips any smaller or more powerful. For that we need new theories of physics. Add to this the fact that the end user is not capable of catching up with what we have innovated so far. In other words, there is a glut of information that end users cannot handle. The industry needs a period of cooling off until the end users catch up with what is available now, and until new physics theories are developed. So what do we do now? We must cut (E), increase (A) to improve cost structure, and move to (P) to offer services in addition to products.

On the margin, Dell apparently cannot improve its cost structure.

What about Dell? In their case the competition has caught up—notebook computers are getting cheaper and cheaper. On the margin, Dell apparently cannot improve its cost structure, its (A). What has made them successful in the past might be the reason for failure in the future. So what to do? Move to services (P) or to innovation (E), such as expanding to include tablets or multi-use devices. This move requires attracting top-level creative people, which Dell probably did not attract in the past since they were squeezing costs to the bone. To be innovative a company needs human capital, which requires a different culture than the cost-cutting, efficiency-oriented one. Cut (A) and increase (E) and (I).

How about Southwest Airlines? It will take a long time for the competition to emulate their culture. There is little danger on that front. But this culture can still be capitalized on. How? By acquiring other airlines and colonializing them with the culture that gives Southwest its competitive advantage.

To strategize for success analyze the industry, analyze the competition, analyze what made you succeed or fail in the past in PAEI terms, and redesign your strategy in PAEI terms for the future.

The Future of Apple, Post-Jobs[1]

ACCORDING TO JEWISH TRADITION, the prophets are gone forever; thus, attempting to predict the future is for the stupid. Nevertheless, since the motto of this blog is "with no fear," I will dare to add my thoughts to the dozens of others in the media about the potential impact of Steve Jobs' departure from Apple. In the analysis that follows, I will use Adizes lingo; otherwise this blog would have to be a book.

Years ago, in 1985, when Jobs was let go (his co-founder, Steve Wozniak, left the company before him), what happened was a predictable, if abnormal and avoidable, syndrome for Apple's stage in its lifecycle: (E)ntrepreneurship was kicked out and replaced by (PA), task-oriented and control-oriented leadership under John Sculley, who went on to almost destroy the company. A (PA) leadership style in a "young" industry is a prescription for a failure. Fortunately, (E) was eventually brought back (Jobs was rehired), and the company regained its position as an innovative leader.

The return of Steve Jobs

This time, Steve Jobs is not being fired. He will remain as Chairman of the Board, which is a lower level of involvement at Apple, and Tim Cook, Apple's COO, is taking his place as the leader.

What do I believe will happen? Not much, for a couple of years. Surely there are lots of Jobs-initiated projects in the pipeline that are still working their way to fruition. But what about two years from now?

High-tech companies are subject to a very high rate of change. It is easy

1. Adizes Insights, September 2011.

for a company that loses its (E) to be overtaken and surpassed by more innovative and aggressive companies.

Why do I say Apple is losing its (E), which has been the source of its phenomenal success? Because it seems to me that the (E) role at Apple was personified by Steve Jobs. Sure, he was not alone in providing entrepreneurial, innovative leadership to the company. But according to reports in the media, he was a very dominating force. He personally would cancel an already finished new product if he did not like it. He personally would abort a project if it did not have the ingredients he approved of.

In (E), not every decision can be articulated or even explained. It is "the taste buds," the intuition, that causes the decision maker to go one way or another. Apparently this intuition was not the result of a team process, which is the way, for instance, the Japanese innovate, as they as individuals are not known to be (E)s.

He personally would cancel an already finished new product if he did not like it.

Who is taking Jobs' place? The former head of operations, who was undoubtedly very good at what he did or he would not have been promoted. But what was he good at? Not (E), because that would have created conflict with Jobs. He was most likely good as Jobs' right hand, working to execute Jobs' strategies, an excellent (PA) who must have had only a minor (E) in his style or he would not have survived under Jobs.

Maybe he is a closet (E) who will come roaring out into the open, but I doubt it. If he were, he would have been very frustrated under Jobs, having his own "taste buds" competing with those of the domineering Jobs.

Look what happened to Applied Materials when Dan Maydan, who was the company's big (E), retired. He was replaced by a (PA), and Applied Materials has been stepping in place ever since. Maydan was replaced by Michael R. Splinter, who had previously been at Intel as Executive Vice President of Sales & Marketing. We know from Adizes Theory that it is wrong to have such a structure because (P) and (E) should not be mixed. When they are, sales orientation, (P), wins and marketing, (E), suffers. Splinter was also General Manager of the Technology and Manufacturing Group, another mix of (P) and (E) where the (P) orientation wins.

My prediction, when he was hired, was that Splinter would cause the exit of any remaining (E) in the company, which is what happened, and Applied Materials has suffered ever since. They stagnated, although the company needs a paradigm shift in its strategy due to the aging of the industry.

At Apple, the situation is not as acute. The new CEO is not coming from the outside. The danger to (E) is not that predictable.

I would be much more comfortable with Apple's future, however, if Jobs had been replaced by the head of marketing or the head of R&D, thus keeping (E) in the leadership position. The fact that this did not happen, I believe, is because these people were minor players to Jobs. He dominated the (E).

Apple's dilemma

What should Apple do now? Apple must institutionalize its (E), something they should have done already: Jobs' departure had been predicted for a long time; his disease was not news to anyone. The company still has time to restructure so that the (E) leadership is provided by the heads of the (E)-function departments. (Unfortunately, I do not know the structure of Apple well enough to name them, but I assume the idea is clear.) Those department heads should report to a single head, thus grouping (E) into a mass that cannot be ignored politically, coached by the chairman of the board, Jobs, while approving or disapproving initiatives.

What company might step into the leading position, replacing Apple in the industry if Apple's (E) is irreplaceable? It is certainly not going to be HP. HP has been losing its indigenous (E) for a very long time, relying on acquisitions to replace its source of innovation. What about Google? Might Google start eyeing this market, now that Apple has lost its main "steering wheel?" Google is not in the hardware business but it has shown an enormous capability to explore markets and technologies in which it has not been the initiator. And just imagine SanDisk and Google getting together....

It is too early to sell Apple short. But I would not buy the stock, either. My recommendation: hold position and see what happens with the (E) role at Apple.

THE PAIN OF BEING THE FOUNDER OF A COMPANY[1]

I HAVE NEW INSIGHTS INTO THE PAIN founders of companies go through when the transition from the founder to the new leader happens.

When the founder started the company no one really bothered him or her. They were the "crazy" ones, working extra hard, overtime, taking risks, ignoring their family and even their health. Who wants that? No one interfered with their decision making or challenged their authority. The work was excessive and the reward questionable; it was not attractive for people to demand participation in decision making.

Now that the company is successful, and there is money, recognition, and respect for the title, everyone and his brother develops an interest in the company and wants to have authority to define its direction. Those under the founder start pushing him out. They want to lead. They want his position.

What is going through his mind is: "Where the hell have you been until now?"

Outgrowing the leader

A struggle for leadership develops, and the replacement is threatening the founder. I have noticed what first triggers the resolve to replace him is that the company has outgrown its founder. By that I mean the company needs some order, not just more growth; not more of the same but better and different.

The founder, having been successful so far, considers these demands for change an affront to his leadership. His ego gets hurt. Furthermore, he is

1. Adizes Insights, June 2012.

getting scared that the recommended changes could destroy what he has built successfully over many years.

He is in pain.

He has experience. He has the scars to prove it. The challengers have lots of energy to push for change because they do not have the same scars. They believe in what they are pushing for and they do not have much to lose. It is not their "baby" that they will lose if what they recommend doing fails.

> *There is glory in building a company but it is followed by pain, deep pain.*

The founder, on the other hand has everything to lose. Years and years of work, hard work, of building the company, paying the price by losing his family, not knowing his children, and maybe even sacrificing his health. To put all of that at risk?

He fights back and is considered a barrier to change. The solution the board of directors comes to or consultants recommend is replacing him.

The second reason that triggers the desire to replace the founder is that he is old and not functioning any more. The company has no energy. It is marching in place while the market is advancing at top speed. The company needs new leadership.

An inconsolable loss

How do you think the founder feels when the demand for replacement comes? Do you think he admits his age? His incapability to lead? He feels used and discarded. His whole life has gone into this company. As one founder told me: "All I remember is when my children were born and when they got married. I have no other memories of my children."

While he has no memories of his children, he remembers every event that happened in the company. Every one of them. And now he is out, goodbye. It would be like raising your children and once they do not need you anymore they send you to an old-age home to die and promise to visit. Depressing, no?

There is glory in building a company but it is followed by pain. Deep pain.

I was consulting to a founder of a company. He had only one daughter, who was taking over the company. They were fighting a lot. What she wanted to do he rejected. And she threatened to quit, which scared him a lot because all these years he believed that he was building this company for the family, for her to grow up and take over.

When we sat in "four eyes" to discuss the situation I asked him how many children he had. He said, surprised at the question, "One. My daughter."

"No," I said. "Two." He got really uncomfortable. This was a religious man and it was like I was going to tell him he had another child out of wedlock. "The second one is the company and you are worried that your daughter will destroy this second child of yours. The second child you devoted more time to than to anyone else."

He started to cry. Really. I touched a nerve.

Starting a company, being a founder, is more than just an entrepreneurial endeavor to make money. You are building a monument to survive your departure from this world, you are building your hall of fame, you are making your dream come true. Now that you are older, and new blood is coming to manage your dream, you are having a nightmare. Are they going to destroy what you have built with so much love?

Is there a way to minimize the pain?

Yes there is, and I have been working on it for forty-four years.

PART VI

�֍

MANAGING

A New Paradigm of Leadership?[1]

I HAVE BEEN OBSERVING OVER THE YEARS how the concept of solving problems for organizations has changed its name. First it was called administration. Thus the first journal in the field was *Administrative Science Quarterly* and schools that were training corporate and organizational leaders were called Graduate Schools of Business *Administration*. The degree granted, MBA, still stands for Master in Business *Administration*.

When the training apparently did not produce the desired results, the concept of administration was relegated to a lower rank within the organization. Administrators just coordinated and supervised, and a new concept was born: management. Gradually at first, and then rapidly, schools changed their name to Graduate School of *Management*.

Apparently that did not work well either, and management was relegated to the middle level of the organization. It lost its appeal and a new word was needed: executive. Graduate programs for *executives* and the concept of Chief Executive Officer was born.

That shift did not produce the desired results either, so once again a new concept emerged: leadership. Books are now published describing how leadership is different from management.

I believe leadership is just another fad. Soon, we will have another word.

We are spinning our wheels, searching for an all-encompassing concept that will cover the roles necessary for running an organization. We are all looking for a model that will describe and identify the specific kind of person who can jumpstart an organization so that it is effective and efficient in both the short and the long run.

1. Adizes Insights, April 2013.

The mistake in this way of thinking lies in the expectation: All the roles are expected to be performed by a single individual, whether he or she is called the administrator, the manager, the executive, or, now, the leader. In reality, one person, even someone extraordinary, can perform only one or, at most, two of the roles required to manage/lead/direct an organization.

For instance, administration focuses on making an organization efficient in the short run. But while administration is necessary, it is also not sufficient if an organization is to perform at the top of its game over the long haul. It's fine when it comes to efficiency, but fails to account for corporate effectiveness. So the verdict on administration: necessary but not sufficient.

The emphasis on management was born to address this deficiency. But management excellence falls short as well. It helps make organizations effective and efficient, but only in the short run. *The ideal executive* The need for long-term effectiveness, for entre- *does not exist.* preneurship, is all too evident.

Enter executive action. Presumably the entrepreneurial executive makes the organization effective in the long run by being proactive. But soon it was recognized that someone needed to rein in the entrepreneur. He was too far out front of the organization. Teamwork is needed and the concept of leadership became the flavor of the day.

The common denominator for all these failing attempts to define the process correctly is a basic one: The paradigm is wrong. The paradigm assumes that a single individual can make any organization function effectively and efficiently in both the short and long run.

It is this notion of individual mastery on which all theories of management are based, whether we call it leadership or management or whatever new word will emerge in the future.

Let me make the point clearly: An individual who can make decisions that will cause an organization to be effective and efficient in the short and long run does not and cannot exist. The roles that produce those results are internally incompatible. The ideal executive does not exist.

In the same way a perfect single parent does not exist. There is no individual who can excel in performing the whole parenting role all by himself or herself. One person alone cannot be both a father and a mother. It takes a family to raise children well. A complementary team. And if for some reason there is a single parent, that person needs an extended family to help raise the child.

A single leader, no matter how functional, will eventually become dysfunctional. Over time, as the organization changes its location on the lifecycle, proceeding from early success to a booming position within the corporate field, that single executive will falter. The qualities that made him or her successful in the past can be the reason for failing in the future. Just like parenting. The style that works when the child is a baby does not necessarily succeed when the child is already mature. The parenting style has to change.

How about changing the leader? It is a solution, but I suggest it is a second-prize choice. Changing leaders is disruptive. It is like having a string of divorces. What is needed is collaborative leadership. Who leads at any point in time depends on what needs to be accomplished.

Look at a functional family. Who leads, husband or wife, depends on what is required at that point in time. The same reasoning holds for companies. To build a company requires a complementary team. It needs collaborative leadership, a team of leaders who differ in their styles but complement each other.

But here is the problem: A complementary team, since it is, by definition, composed of different styles, generates conflict. So although conflict is good, although it is necessary and indispensable for good leadership and good management, it can be destructive and dysfunctional.

What is needed to avoid this potential dysfunctional and destructive conflict is collaborative leadership based on mutual trust and respect.

Collaborative leadership will work only if it is really collaborative, which means that there is mutual trust and respect.

Our management development programs and training of future managers (or leaders, or executives) are all based on the wrong paradigm. They concentrate on individualism when what is needed is to train people how to work in complementary teams, to harness conflict with mutual trust and respect.

We are still trying to develop and train and create this elusive perfect executive/manager/leader. It cannot happen. It will not happen. It has never happened. Our management education needs revamping. It needs to be re-engineered. And our managerial leadership culture needs redirecting as well.

Dreams That Turn into Nightmares[1]

I AM CONSULTING TO THE KIBBUTZ MOVEMENT of Israel. Kibbutzim (plural for kibbutz) were established with a Communist ideology that Russian Jewish settlers brought with them at the beginning of the twentieth century.

Here it is how it is supposed to work. No one owns anything. It is all communal property. The community provides all you need: housing, food, health, education. Members work, and if they work outside the kibbutz they bring all their earnings to the community chest. Each member gets a monthly stipend based on how many children the family has, regardless of how much he or she contributed. The stipend is minimal, just enough for some travel to the city, some clothes, and some toys for the kids.

Like a very traditional family

It reminds me of very traditional families like those of Jews from Halleb, Syria, or the Albanian family structures in the Balkans. The father owns it all. The children work in the family business and contribute differently, but their allotment, or salary, from the family business is the same unless they have different number of children.

One kibbutz member established a company, which employs people from outside the kibbutz. It has over 2,000 employees worldwide, and over a billion dollars in revenues per year. And what does the founder get? Nothing more than a member of the kibbutz who washes dishes. He has no equity in the business and no extra rights. If his children want to

1. Adizes Insights, May 2012.

get an expensive university education, they have to be approved by the economic committee of the kibbutz like any other children.

The kibbutz system has interesting problems, like family businesses do. The dream of equality, common interest, and mutual respect is a nightmare for some.

There is no such thing as equality in a system like this. It is the reverse of equality because some work harder—much, much harder—than others but get the same food, the same housing, and the same monthly stipend. This is especially unfair for those who accepted the responsibility of being leaders, managers, in a kibbutz. They work extra hard, have their decisions criticized by the membership, have responsibilities that keep them awake at night, and nevertheless receive no extra recognition or benefits.

This brings me to the insight that hierarchy is a necessary evil.

There is another phenomenon similar to fights that occur in family businesses if there is no strong parent who keeps the family toeing the line: internal gossip, backstabbing, and nonstop criticism. Since there is no "strong parent" in a kibbutz the members behave like a dysfunctional family.

It cannot be eliminated. Rejecting it for ideological reasons does not mean it ceases to exist. It will be created informally. There is a need for a leader, because the pain that informal inequality generates needs to be handled by someone. It needs to be directed at someone or the members will attack each other. (In other words, the political theory that supports anarchy is not a workable system.)

A manager has a role that I have not seen in the literature: to be hated from time to time. This needs to happen because when a person feels wronged he or she needs to blame someone for the pain he or she is feeling. If there is no leadership figure to absorb the hard feelings, to take them on, they do not disappear; they get directed at the community at large.

The kibbutz is changing. It has to.

On Equality[1]

EQUALITY WAS ONE OF THE THREE famous rallying cries of the French Revolution, the others being liberty and fraternity.

Equality has been a goal of numerous political and social movements, Communism among them. "All people are born equal" had in it the assumption that if people are born equal, they should remain so. Inequality to them is an anomaly.

The kibbutz movement in Israel, which I am advising now, has always had equality as a cornerstone of its philosophy. And it is a cornerstone of many religious movements, as well. I consulted to such an organization years ago: Kripalu, a US yoga spiritual center. The Catholic Church, to whom the Adizes Institute consults today, has many orders whose members commit to equality, poverty, and service.

I encountered something similar in consulting to some Jewish families originally from Halleb, Syria. The brothers in the family work as hard as they know how, earn as much as they can, but share equally, regardless of how much each of them has contributed. The same is true in traditional Albanian families.

But, how does it work? *Does* it work?

A struggle for dominance

First, we should realize that there is no equality in nature. Look at animals; there is a clear hierarchy. But the same holds for humans. Look at your children: Don't they fight for the toy their sibling is holding, even if an identical toy is sitting on the floor next to them? If they want equality

1. Adizes Insights, June 2012.

there it is: two toys, exactly the same. So why are they fighting? For dominance. For a position on the totem pole, in the hierarchy. Not for equality.

A hierarchy is one of the causes of inequality. Since hierarchy cannot be avoided, nor can it be eliminated either legally or politically, since it is a natural-phenomenon, inequality cannot be eliminated either.

When equality is forced, in income levels for instance, in order to return to the natural state of inequality, inequality in non-pecuniary differentials will appear with extra force. Status will become more important than when there are income differentials. And if equality is forced both in income levels and in status, somehow the dynamics of the social interactions will find a way to bring the system to its natural state of inequality.

A hierarchy is one of the causes of inequality.

Take the kibbutz example. In my opinion, the insistence on equality in the monthly allowance for each member, as well as the insistence on the principle that leaders get no more recognition than anyone else, is causing much of the internal discord, even backstabbing, that characterizes some kibbutzim. Inequality is created by the negative feedback people give each other. They put themselves up by putting others down.

A condition for finding a solution, I believe, is to first emancipate ourselves from a utopian expectation of equality. We should accept that there is no possible operational equality and there cannot be, always and forever. Instead, we should be vigilant in ensuring that the inequality, at any point in time, is not hopeless: The "losers" should not perceive the inequality as impossible to overcome, that there is no future opportunity to be equal, even through multi-generational efforts.

In the meantime what to do? What is a workable inequality?

Income differences

Regarding income differences, I found from experience that a multiple of seven is tolerable: The top person in the organization does not earn more than seven times what the lowest-paid person in the same organization earns. A multiple of five is not only acceptable but recognized as being legitimate. A multiple of three is tolerable, but not sustainable; it will discourage people from taking leadership positions.

I found out, again from experience, that those multiples work not only in financial terms, in income, but also for non-pecuniary rewards such as recognition and status symbols. For example, when structuring companies with the Adizes Methodology, we insist on no more than seven layers in the organizational structure, regardless of how big the company is. (The largest company we ever restructured was a multi-national company with 250,000 employees.) I also insisted on this principle in designing a structure for the armed forces of a country: From private to the chief of staff, there should be no more than seven ranks. (Unfortunately, the client did not accept the principle, and the result has been an increasingly bureaucratic military establishment.)

How about a family structure? Obviously, children are not equal to parents. But what about equality between the parents? Women have been demanding equality in all aspects of running family life. But in reality, has equality been achieved, or has a new and different but still unequal balance been established? I have noted a burgeoning movement of men demanding equality, because, for instance, they feel that women are increasingly getting preferential treatment from courts in divorce cases.

The multiple principle will not work here. No one is on salary and there is no such thing as a multiple in recognition. What to do?

A workable inequality

With some effort, a workable inequality can be achieved in a dynamic way. In certain areas of life, one party will have more than the other. For instance, the cosmetic needs of women exceed the cosmetic needs (so far) of men. So be it. At the same time, men's need for gadgets exceeds that of most women. (Please do not take this differentiation literally. Of course it is sometimes true that a woman wants more gadgets and a man more cosmetics. What is important is that there is give and take. The principle will obviously not work if one of the parties wants more of everything, in every arena, than the other party gets.)

How about the hierarchy in decision making? A workable solution is that on some issues the wife has final authority, while the husband has final authority on others. The decision about who has final authority on which issues should be negotiated.

There are extreme situations where "equality" is a social, political, or religious requirement, a value statement that is forced. I found it can work (more or less) but it requires a very strong parent or leader, who is accepted unequivocally by all the stakeholders, who ensures that the natural forces of inequality are dealt with, one who instills religious, political, or social pressures to overcome the natural tendency for inequality.

In the case of the kibbutzim, in the past, when Israel was being established, the dual ideologies of Communism and Zionism temporarily created a unifying force that obviated the need for a "parent" to solve the problems caused by forcing people into an unnatural environment requiring total equality.

That unifying ideology did not last. The country was established and the Israeli pioneering society has been replaced by rampant materialism, and the kibbutzim inside that society that are still trying to live by the principles of equality are in serious crisis. Some have dissolved utterly, while others have become somewhat privatized and continue to struggle with how to define "equality," and, indeed, how to define "kibbutz," under these new organizational principles.

The goal should not be equality in results. It is not natural. The goal should be equality in opportunities. The inequality in results should be carefully managed by the leadership of that system, in order not to become dysfunctional. At the minimum, leadership must provide hope that the inequality can be overcome.

SELF-FULFILLING PROPHECIES[1]

IF YOU IMAGINE ON YOUR WAY HOME that you will have a fight with your wife, when you arrive home and she opens the door, you are already so worked up arguing with her in your head that it is very probable you will bark at her as soon as she opens the door. And guess what: There will be a fight. You predicted it. You caused it.

I have been thinking that this illumination has repercussions for investing in the stock market. Do not study the trends. Do not try to predict the economy. You are opening the wrong door.

> *You are opening the wrong door.*

Read what the various gurus predict is going to happen to the market. If there is a consensus that the market will go up you can bet it will. Why? Because if people believe the gurus that the market is going to go up they will start buying stock, and as they buy more and more, guess what? The stock market will go up. A self-fulfilling prophecy.

That is what is happening to the New York real estate market. The newspapers, the media (which can be manipulated), projected an upswing in real estate prices. And what has happened? People started raising the prices for their properties, and voila: the real estate prices go up.

What you project—if you believe in it enough—will actually happen. If we, as a society, believe in it together we make it happen, too. If we believe that global warming will happen, it is bound to occur. But if we are convinced we can stop it, our mass inclination will prevail.

What occurs in our personal life follows what we individually believe is going to happen, while what occurs in communal life follows what we

1. Adizes Insights, May 2013.

jointly believe as a community. Why would I personally try to cut the emissions of my car if I believe no one else will, or not enough people will do so to make a difference?

This has repercussions for leaders and leadership. Our leaders and heads of state need to project hope and trust, and, in the process, build a communal expectation that what is desired will actually happen.

Even if you do not believe it, as a leader you must project belief and expectation if you want change to occur.

Leadership is not designed to reinforce where we are coming from, but rather to project confidently where we should be heading.

Similarities Between the Human Body and Organizations[1]

D R. LOUIS TEULIERES, a French doctor of medicine who specializes in alternative medicine, and I have been comparing notes. We found many similarities between the human body and organizations as it pertains to PAEI.

Like an organization, the human body aims to be effective and efficient in the short and long run, and the PAEI roles can be identified within functions performed in the body. For instance the adrenal gland provides the (P) role. The thyroid—the mobilizer, the activator—the (E) role. The pituitary gland controls the thyroid; that is your (A).

There are neuro-mediators that also perform the PAEI roles: dopamine the (P) role; gamma-Aminobutyric acid, or GABA, the (A) role; serotonin the (I) role.

As Dr. Teulieres described to me people who have too much GABA, I was finishing his sentences. He was describing a bureaucrat.

The activity of the glands changes over a person's lifecycle. Here he and I also found commonalities. With a baby, the thyroid is very active, much more so than the adrenal gland. In adolescence the pituitary gland's activity goes up and the thyroid's down.

This was a confirmation for me that the growth of (A) in organizational adolescence should not be at the expense of (P)—as I have claimed for years, described and prescribed in my book on lifecycles, but about which I was having doubts—but rather at the expense of (E). First, because (E) precedes (P), (E) should decline before (P); and second, and even more important, that is what happens in reality. That is what was happening in organizations everywhere, and my fighting it was not working. This

1. Adizes Insights, December 2010, by Ichak Kalderon Adizes Ph.D. and Louis Teulieres MD.

means there is a reason for this behavior, and the human body analogy confirmed it for me.

Also interesting to note was that GABA and serotonin are inversely related: More GABA means less serotonin, and vice versa. That confirms the inverse relation between (I) and (A).

Another point: When people get older they seek more serotonin, more (I). They like more sugar and chocolate. And women, who are typically more (I) oriented, love sugar and chocolate more than men. Older people are not so much after meat; they do not seek much (P). In aging, (P) goes down.

An even more exciting insight from our interaction was the following:

The system manages itself.

As we were discussing how the different parts of the body perform the PAEI functions, he said, "There is no chief, no one organ that manages it all."

What about the brain, I thought to myself. Aha! There is no one brain. There is the left brain, where the (PA) roles are performed, and the right brain, where the (EI) roles are performed.

So what manages the totality?

No one. The system manages itself.

It is a system in which every part performs its role well. That is Socrates' definition of a perfect system.

Every part has a function that, in totality, comprises a structure and there is a predetermined functioning between the parts, i.e., a process. The system is both synergetic (jointly the parts create growth) and symbiotic (having a mutually benefiting interdependency).

What makes the system healthy is the ease with which energy flows between the parts.

What should the analogy be for organizational management? The role of management is to establish the system and see to it that the system functions symbiotically and synergistically. When it does not function well, it is management's role to fix it.

We have to be conscious when some parts of the body do not function well, when the energy does not flow well, when we are sick and take measures to heal ourselves. Not by chemicals (not by consultants), but by creating an environment in which the body can take care of itself and heal itself.

That is the Adizes training and development programs, where we create an environment and teach how to operate in it, where the parts of the organization heal themselves and thus heal the organization.

The role of management is "to create an environment where the most desirable will most probably happen," to quote the CEO of Ogden Corporation from many years back.

Management's role is to be the thumb, to enable the other four fingers to act as a hand.

THE DIMENSION OF TIME—WHAT IS IT?[1]

BJARNI SNÆBJÖRN JÓNSSON, a doctoral candidate from Iceland at the Adizes Graduate School for the Study of Change and Leadership, pointed out to me to an interesting finding. Here it is in his own words:

> During the writing of my dissertation I came to study the Norse mythology in relation to the concept of collective intelligence (wisdom) and especially the concept of fate. Fate was linked to the way the Vikings felt accountable for their actions. In the mythology there were three witches of fate: Urdur (past), Verdandi (present), and Skuld (Future). Verdandi (present) was always accompanied by either Urdur (past) or Skuld (future), which represents the view that what you did in the present was a result of something you did in the past, which you carried with you into the future. The meaning of the name of the future witch, Skuld, means debt, representing the debt you carried into the future depending on your actions in the present.

> For the Vikings, time was an endless continuum where the being in the present was more of a space or dimension, rather than a sort of isolated time slot; you were living in a space of time which was all-encompassing of past, present, and future.

I have been saying essentially the same thing in my lectures without realizing the Vikings said it a thousand years ago. The present is either the continuation of your past or the beginning of your future. It, in itself, does not exist. It is a fraction of a second continuing the past, or a fraction of a second beginning the future.

Moreover, do you realize that in the present you are thinking and debating with the voice in your head about something that happened in

1. Adizes Insights, December 2013.

the past? You are de facto reliving your past in the present. Minutes or even seconds later you might switch to elaborate about your future in your thoughts; you live your future in your present.

Imagine having an argument in your head with someone you are going to see. When you arrive, you start arguing with that person in a manner you could say is a continuation of the argument you had with that person in your head in the past.

Often psychologists tell you your present fight with your spouse is not really with your spouse. She represents some unresolved fight you had, say, with a parent in the past, which you are now reenacting in the present.

The present is either the continuation of your past or the beginning of your future.

Have you ever experienced something that made you wonder, did I not have this experience before? Past and future seem to be all mixed into our present. The time dimension is a space that encompasses present, past, and future.

The Eastern philosophies, picked up by New Age gurus, tell us to live in the present, which means to divorce our mind of discussing the past or living in the future. According to this philosophy, it is the only way for the present to emerge; otherwise you really do not know what is happening right now.

What are the repercussions for us today?

When you ask some people what is going on now they will reply, "We are doing such and so." But listen carefully and you will realize they are describing what they have been doing so far, i.e., in the past. Ask others the same question and they will describe what they are starting to do different for the future.

For those of the (A) style, my observation is that they view the present as continuation of the past, and the (E)s see it as the beginning of the future. That explains to me why they do not necessarily agree or even like each other.

It reflects also on the political orientation of liberals (the present is the beginning of the future) versus conservatives (the present is the continuation of the past).

The understanding that past and future are all molded into our present should make us less judgmental of ourselves. What is happening in the present was not born in the present. It is the result of actions taken in the past, maybe even in past lives. Much of what we do today is driven by our past and thus it is not strange we do not always understand our actions in the present.

We should take responsibility for what we do in the present because the repercussions will face us in the future. As to the past we cannot correct it. Only learn from it in order to not repeat the mistakes in the present.

WHY BEING TOO GOOD
MIGHT BE TOO BAD[1]

IN MY CONSULTING PRACTICE I often came across a certain experience that I felt highly opinionated about. Today, I fully disagree with my previous conclusions.

People would inform me that they were recently fired and were, obviously, very upset. "I worked so hard," they would tell me. "Sixty hours or more per week. When they fired me, they had to replace me with three people. And what is the reward for my hard work, for saving the company money, doing the working of three people and getting the salary of one? I get fired!"

I used to feel for the person and judge the company, not only for its heartlessness but also because it seemed to be a poor managerial decision to fire such an outstanding, hard-working, and loyal employee. Now that I have experienced having to fire such an employee, I have a different perspective.

Which kind of managerial style do you believe will work sixty hours a week? A (P)roducer, right? And why is this person continuously working such long hours? Because this person's style is that of a Lone Ranger who does not delegate. He needs all work to go through him, requiring him to work very long hours. So when the Lone Ranger is fired, three people have to take this person's job. It was a task meant for three people, yet he insisted on doing it all by himself.

Do you believe he was doing a good job? No! Things fell through the cracks. Many tasks missed their deadline because he was just too busy. He was juggling too many balls in the air when he could only hold one ball at a time.

1. Adizes Insights, August 2010.

(P)s are linear in their behavior. They want to do everything, but their style is to do one thing at a time, which means all other assignments get neglected. They do not prioritize well. They pay attention to the squeakiest wheel first, putting aside significant tasks for later and addressing them only when they become a crisis.

Would you keep such an employee, especially if this person was in a managerial position? This person is a dangerous bottleneck who is costing you far more than the salary you pay him because of the damage their style is causing. "But they work hard," someone might argue. You want the people who work for you to work intelligently, not just hard.

> *You want the people who work for you to work intelligently.*

"But replacing this person with three other people costs more money," someone might say. Not so. Since this person is a bottleneck you probably consider him indispensable, so to keep him going you have given him salary increases and bonuses. He might be way overpaid for the formal position he holds. Add to that the cost of mistakes, decisions not followed up on in a timely manner, and the loss of productivity by others waiting for the bottleneck to process decisions, and you might find out that this person is way, way too expensive to keep. You might find that replacing him with three competent individuals working normal hours actually makes you more money.

My recommendation is to watch out for people who work too hard and are indispensable. They cost you money, not *save* you money.

ABOUT THE ADIZES INSTITUTE

FOR THE PAST FORTY years, the Adizes Institute has been committed to equipping visionary leaders, management teams, and agents of change to become champions of their industries and markets. These leaders have successfully established a collaborative organizational culture by using Adizes' pragmatic tools and concepts to achieve peak performance.

Adizes specializes in guiding leaders of organizations (CEOs, top management teams, boards, owners) to quickly and effectively resolve such issues as:

- Difficulties in executing good decisions.
- Making the transition from entrepreneurship to professional management.
- Difficulties in aligning the structure of the organization to achieve its strategic intent.
- Bureaucratizing—the organization is getting out of touch with its markets and beginning to lose entrepreneurial vitality.
- Conflicts among founders, owners, board members, partners, and family members.
- Internal management team conflicts and "politics" severe enough to inhibit the success of the business.
- Growing pains.
- Culture clashes between companies undergoing mergers or acquisitions.

Adizes also offers comprehensive training and certification for change leaders who wish to incorporate into their practice the Adizes Methodologies for managing change.

Adizes is the primary sponsor of the Adizes Graduate School, a nonprofit teaching organization that offers Master's and Ph.D. programs for the Study of Leadership and Change.

For more information about these and other programs, please visit www.adizes.com.

Adizes
INSTITUTE WORLDWIDE